The

SIXAREEN

and

HER RACING DESCENDANTS

by

CHARLES SANDISON

The Shetland Times Ltd.
Lerwick

1994

ISBN 0 900662 99 9

First published by
T. & J. Manson, Lerwick, 1954.
This facsimile edition published by
The Shetland Times Ltd., 1994.

All royalties from this publication to be paid to the
Unst Boat Haven

British Library Cataloguing-in-Publication Data
A catalogue record for this book is available from the British Library

Printed and published by The Shetland Times Ltd.,
Prince Alfred Street, Lerwick, Shetland ZE1 0EP.

To the memory of

The Haaf Fishermen of Shetland,
and the fine boats they sailed.

"They that go down to the sea in ships,
that do business in great waters;
These see the works of the Lord,
and his wonders in the deep".

Psalm CVII.

CONTENTS

LIST OF ILLUSTRATIONS

PHOTOGRAPHS

DIAGRAMS

INTRODUCTION AND ACKNOWLEDGMENT

IT is a commonplace that only after a thing is irretrievably past and gone do we begin to see it in its true perspective and to value it as a landmark in progress; and so it is with the sixareens of Shetland. Their disappearance towards the end of last century was hardly noticed.

The advent of the much larger "Buckie boats", or scaffies, from the Moray Firth had sealed their fate, and in turn these scaffies themselves were quickly replaced by the fine fifies and zulus of the East Coast. With their huge unstayed masts, great lug sails, and wonderful sailing qualities, these boats were ideal for the rising herring industry, which rapidly eclipsed the line fishing in importance.

In the early years of this century as many as 750 of these boats have been engaged to fish here, and on the first Sunday of June each displayed a great coloured streamer from her foremast, and made a wonderfully gay scene: 1500 masts and 750 flags lining the two sides of the harbour, with a background of thousands upon thousands of herring barrels built up along the shores, and acres upon acres of green grass covered by brown fishing nets, each "fleet" with its 60 or so individual nets laid neatly one on the other with the sixty rows of corks spaced three or four feet apart.

You could walk the length of either side of the voe on nets, or on the boats themselves, so closely were they packed.

And yet I have never seen a photograph of one of these great luggers really stepping out. How fast could she go? How close to the wind could she sail and at what speed?

I have heard of one of these boats tearing into Baltasound in half a gale, with her foresail at the masthead and a great bone in her teeth, a late arrival from the Coast carrying on to the astonishment of her compatriots who had already arrived at this northern port. But the name of the boat, her skipper, and the time of her record-breaking voyage from Troup Head is lost. Yet it must have been remarkable for the story to be recounted to me many years after the event.

It is not to be wondered that the open sixareen vanished from the seas in the space of little more than a decade in the face of such an imposing display of power. With the help of the steam capstan each of these luggers would have nearly ten times the fishing capacity of a sixareen, and yet she required a crew that was no larger.

It is on the small racing craft of Shetland, and on the "eela boats", that the survival of the sixareen model largely depends, and there is good evidence that not only will it survive but that its popularity is spreading even outside these Islands.

Many of these were fitted with small engines and used in the war of 1939-45, and more are still being built. They make splendid little motor boats.

I have introduced a chapter on speed and "speed roses" as the most practical way of showing what these boats can do, and of comparing the performance of different sizes of boat.

This is a matter that receives little attention from yachtsmen generally, because the object of racing is to beat your opponent rather than to calculate the exact speed in knots that this will require in an infinite variety of racing conditions—indeed a quite impossible task.

Nevertheless we surely owe it to a good boat or yacht, particularly one of unusual type, to "tell the world" something of what may be expected from her, and for this purpose the most appropriate "yardstick" seems to be that of critical-speed where displacement craft are concerned.

Perhaps it is not possible in these days of semi-planing hulls to draw a hard and fast line between displacement and planing craft.

Perhaps also these Shetland boats may at times have tended to plane, and the term "sea-loose" that was sometimes applied in the case of sixareens does suggest this. But we must have some basis of comparison, and the critical speed based on waterline length serves the purpose well in comparing these boats with one another.

It is neccessary to emphasise the importance that was placed on speed, even in the fishing sixareens: speed under sail, and perhaps even more speed when rowed. This racing was a matter of honour rather than of profit, but it took a very high place in developing the hull form of these boats. Incidentally the careful modelling of the under-water body which this would involve would also make the boat more seaworthy.

In fact from her earliest ancestors speed with sea-worthiness has been the chief aim of the craftsman who fashioned these open boats, and this is still the aim of the builders of her racing descendants.

In what follows I will attempt to show the close connections between Norway and the Shetland Islands from the ninth to the nineteenth centuries, and how this largely controlled the type of open boat used for fishing in the Islands up to about 1820; how the sixareen as we know her evolved as an independent model in the early decades of last century, and why her racing descendants of today still adhere to the sixareen model.

In matters relating to sixareens much was learned from that well known builder, Robert Nicolson of Haraldswick, who built 100 boats large and small in his time, and to others of his generation who fished in them as young men.

My thanks are due to Dr Manson of Lerwick for permission to quote from the wonderful description of the great storm of 1881 written by Charles Johnson of Toam; to Mr Ratter of Lerwick for photographs of sixareens at Feideland; to Mr Plenderleith of the Royal Scottish Museum for photographs and particulars of models; to Mr Johannestjern for measurements of two of the longships preserved at Bygdoy; and to Mr Williamson of Skerries and Messrs Ratter and Sinclair of Cullivoe for accounts of fast coastal passages in sixareens.

Hamar,
Baltasound, 1953.

Chapter I.

THE VIKING ROAD

"And the men that breed from them
They traffic up and down,
But cling to their cities' hem
As a child to the mother's gown";

Kipling.

THE North Isles of Shetland lie right across the old Viking route to the North West, and must have been a convenient stepping-stone to the more distant islands of the north Atlantic. In fact these islands and the Faroes lie in a direct line from southern Norway to Iceland.

On sailing straight into the setting sun from the island of Feje, at the northern end of Hjelte Fjord (Shetland Fjord), and one of the main approaches to Bergen, the Viking fishing bank would be passed at 60 to 70 miles, and the island of Balta reached at 160 miles. If the Holmengraa Skerries of Norway are excluded this is the point at which the British Isles most nearly approach Scandinavia.

Compared with the long sea passages the Viking rovers were accustomed to make this crossing was a short and easy journey, just a stepping-stone to the edge of the continental shelf and the mysteries that lay beyond.

Sixareen Yacht of 1939 on the "Viking Road"

This road to the north west passed between the three large northern islands of Unst, Fetlar and Yell. Approaching from the east and with a good landfall at Strandbrough in Fetlar this island was kept to port, and the small islands of Daey, Urie Lingey, Sound Gruney and Linga on the same side. To starboard were the small islands of Haaf Gruney, Wedder Holm, Uyea and Holm of Heogland, where the narrows of Blumel Sound with its six-knot tide were entered, and so out to the Atlantic Ocean.

There was much to recommend this route with its ten-mile stretch of sheltered water, clean beaches and sheltered bays where their ships could anchor or be beached in safety, and where they could doubtless augment their store of provisions from the comparatively flat and fertile lands on either side.

Near either end of this stretch of sheltered water, but in each case facing the open sea, are the remains of the Norse settlements at Easting in Unst and Brecken in Yell, facing east and north-west respectively.

Compared with the advantages of this route the alternative of passing north of Unst was not attractive. Here the land presents precipitous cliffs to the ocean, and the latter is disturbed by what the old cartographers describe as "A Cruel Rost, or Tydgart". This graphic description was surely written after a rounding of the most northerly rocks in Britain in indifferent weather conditions! That it does no more than justice to this particular tide race the following incident will show.

About seventeen years ago a steam trawler of 120 feet or so in length put into Baltasound for shelter, and people rubbed their eyes on seeing a barrel of cod roe jammed between mizzen shrouds and mast. It looked like a mischievous trick, and so it was—a trick of the sea. No man could have got the barrel there. What had happened was this. The trawler was running before a north-west gale from the Faroe fishing grounds, and rounding the north of Unst was pooped by a great hollow sea. From the high wheelhouse they looked down on a welter of foaming water and thought that the vessel had gone. There was literally nothing to be seen aft but the engineroom casing and mizzen mast above a smother of broken water and foam. Even the lifeboat stowed on crutches on the after deck was smothered. However, gradually the water poured off over the sides and through the scuppers and the lifeboat appeared, still lashed securely down, but the barrel of cod roe was gone. It was jammed between mizzen and shrouds some 15 feet above the deck! This and three feet of water in the cabin was all the damage.

To get a clear picture of how remote islands such as these could figure so prominently in the history of a nation it is necessary to remember that the quickest and easiest means of transport was by ships on the sea. This must have been so from the dawn of history right up to the advent of the steam train. For a maritime nation there were no roads to be made. The sea was there and could be traversed in any direction at will, and men and material moved more freely than by any other method. Fleets of up to 1200 craft are mentioned in the Sagas.

But storms and contrary winds had to be reckoned with and food and water provided, so that any island that could provide shelter or food was useful. If it could provide both it would be like an oasis to the desert traveller, and if it also happened to lie near a main route it would naturally become a rendezvous for traffic on that route. This is just what Shetland was for the Viking rovers from Norway, as later it became to the Dutch fleets in search of herring.

Travelling by long-ship Shetland was only two days' journey from Bergen, even by oar, and if there was a good sailing wind this time might almost be halved. Fine lined vessels like these of over sixty feet would easily maintain a steady seven knots with a fresh leading wind. So for the Vikings Shetland had the great advantage of lying on the direct route to Iceland and being at the same time a convenient rendezvous for raids on either coast of Scotland. No doubt it also formed a safe retreat if the raid did not go according to plan.

Haraldswick in Unst gets its name from the landing reported to have been made there by Harald Fairhair when he set out to subdue the recalcitrant chiefs who had fled to these islands rather than submit to his rule in Norway, and who were now commencing to retaliate by raids on Norway itself. On this expedition he probably followed this north route to Shetland. Tradition says that he tried to land at Funzie, three miles south of Strandbrough in Fetlar, but finding the bay unsuitable for his ships turned northwards and landed at Haraldswick where there are two wide "ayres" of exactly the kind described in the Olaf Trygvisson Saga as used for landing and hauling out ships. A great battle was fought here and Harald was supposed to have been killed in the nearby Heogs hills at a place still known as "King Harald's Grave". History states, however, that he lived to a good old age and was buried at Hauge in Karmtsund north of Stavanger about 936.

Harald subdued Orkney and Shetland and appropriated to the crown of Norway all the waste lands, and once a year the king's tax gatherer came to Urie in Fetlar to collect the tax, or "scat".

Urie lies right on the viking route through the North Isles and would be a convenient centre for this purpose. Half an hour's sail would take him from Urie to the centre of the eighteen-mile long island of Yell, with its two deep voes which run far into the island. Unst is the same distance away. In fact, for an official with a long-ship at his disposal, travel throughout the whole three northern islands must have been quite as convenient as it is today.

Over these same waters the descendants of these ships now run their races: sliding gunter and jib, or the Shetland square-sail.

About 600 years later Shetland was pledged as part of the dowry of Princess Margaret of Denmark on her marriage to James III. of Scotland in 1469, and the islands came under the Scottish Crown, but it appears to have been 1611 before a serious attempt was made to establish the laws of Scotland exclusively in the islands.

One hundred and fifty years later, four-oared and six-oared boats were being imported from Bergen in large numbers, together with other fishing requirements such as lines and hooks, timber and tar, and even luxury goods such as tobacco and spirits: twenty hogshead of best French brandy in one shipment!

Even in 1820 built boats were still being imported from Bergen, along with boat sets in shaped boards and pieces, and the latter practice at least continued for some years so that up to about 1830 the Shetland fishing boat would exactly duplicate her opposite number in Norway.

It seems probable, therefore, that the birth of the Sixareen as an independent Shetland model took place in the first half of last century.

This period too saw the first regular connection between Shetland and Scotland, by sailing boat when weather permitted, and by 1840 a regular summer service by steamer, giving the Shetland boatbuilder access to Scottish larch for planking as an alternative to timber from Norway.

Meantime the herring fishing was beginning to assume local importance, and in the latter half of the century there was a seasonal influx of fisher-folk and boats from Scotland. These boats fished from Lerwick and "out-stations" scattered all over the islands, so that after something like 1100 years from the time of the first influx of Norse colonists the Scandinavian influence came to an end. Contact with Norway concerning fishing craft, apart from whaling, ceased to be of importance to the Islands, while that with Scotland became paramount.

With the advent of steam, too, the old Viking route to the north-west passed into the realm of history. Today the service from Bergen passes 10 miles north of Unst, and that from Denmark south of Shetland altogether, so that as a stopping place on the route Shetland has ceased to be of importance.

In the last twenty-seven years, however, two expeditions have set out from Norway to follow the Viking route. First the "Leif Erikson", named after Leif son of Erik the Red who was supposed to be the first Norseman to set foot on American soil about the year 986 A.D. She anchored in Cullivoe for a night before setting out for Iceland, but must have met with disaster, as she was never heard of again.

The second expedition was undertaken in a ship of the old long-ship type, complete with a square-sail but with the most valuable addition of a motor. She followed the same track between the North Isles of Shetland and also anchored in Cullivoe. In fact she created something of a sensation when she appeared sailing in from the east with the morning sun behind her and her great striped square-sail billowing out with the breeze.

After such a long period of Norse influence, it can hardly be wondered at that Norse place names and words are so prominent in the Islands, and that up to fifty years ago words relating to boats, fishing and the sea were almost exclusively Old Norse. In fact, at the haaf fishing English names were taboo.

As recently as 70 years ago there were old people living in the north of Unst who could remember hearing, as children, their parents using a language which they did not understand. This was the Norn dialect, and Dr. Jakobsen of Copenhagen who visited Shetland from 1893 to 1895 and made a study of this subject states that some 10,000 words derived from the Norn still survived in the islands.

So it happened that for a very long period both circumstances and similarity of interest favoured the retention of the Norway boats, and even when circumstances changed towards the end of the period, as long as open boats were used for the haaf-fishing in Shetland they remained true to type. Even today the model is still universally favoured for all open craft.

BALTA SOUND — 946 A.D.

The Sound was a welcome haven on the storm tossed northern sea,
Where the long-ships scud for shelter, in the isle of Balta's lee.
And the mists of bygone ages, saw reared stone by stone,
On its rocky, northern shore, a banished Norseman's home.

Look from its upper windows, when the Sound is crested white,
And the angry hollow combers roll onwards in their might.
See the shoals of Swarta Skerry reach out and bar their way—
Then turn and look below you to the shelter of the bay.

Look from the house in summer to the sparkling sea, and the land,
And the emerald green of the water over by Skeotaing sand:
The islands in the back ground, and the "stringing" of the tide
From Beacon to Giv of Hunie, and on to the ocean wide.

Now a thousand years have passed, since first the Vikings came,
And gave us names like "Skiphoul", "Ordel", "Houb" and "Hame".
And the flood at the "noost" still covers the shingle that ground their keels,
And over the moving waters, still the greater black-back wheels.

1946 A.D.

What be those ships at anchor: near by the Balta shore,
Where the long-ships lay in that bygone day,
As told in the old folk-lore?
They be modern ships of Norway, bound for their own homeland,
And like their sires of a thousand years
They shelter by Balta's sand!

Note:—Many Norwegian fishing vessels crossed to this country during the war, and on 1st January, 1946, a flotilla of these, homeward bound, and escorted by naval vessels, put into Baltasound for the night.

Chapter II.

THE ANCESTRY OF THE SIXAREEN

"The boat too, was something more than a boat.
She had come sailing out from the long distant ages;
She had once been a Viking ship . . . . . "

Johan Bojer, *The Last of the Vikings.*

THE extremely close association between Shetland and the Scandinavian countries from the middle of the ninth to the middle of the fifteenth century, and the continuing trade contacts right up to the early years of the last century, particularly in maritime matters, have already been mentioned.

That the Islands were also useful stepping-stones to the north-west has also been shown. This alone would mean a fairly steady service of vessels touching at the Islands on journeys to and from Scandinavia from more distant lands. In fact, up to the beginning of last century the quickest way of getting to Scotland was sometimes *via* Denmark or Holland.

By the eighties of last century Swedish fishing boats for cod and ling were coming to Shetland in considerable numbers. At first they were small sailing vessels, with high bows and broad beam, and as they fished largely to the west and north-west of Shetland they made Baltasound their headquarters. They were not great sailers and their safety in rough weather depended on anchoring at sea and riding it out. For this purpose they were equipped with a very long and heavy "grass" rope, made, it was said, by their women-folk.

When steam replaced sail for the Hull and Grimsby trawlers towards the end of last century, many of these fine sailing ketches were bought by Sweden and began to appear in increasing numbers in Shetland waters. Up to one hundred have been counted in Baltasound alone, and here a Mission Church was opened by the Church of Sweden. It is still in use today but recently Norwegian fishers, particularly shark fishers, have been here in greater numbers than the Swedes.

These Scandinavian types, however, arrived too late to have any influence at all on the sixareen of the North Isles of Shetland, as the last of these were built in the closing years of last century. The same applies to the tremendous "invasion" of harbours round the islands by Scottish herring fishing boats, mostly big herring luggers, and fine sailers, who often brought north with them roomy straight-stemmed open row-boats, and small decked zulus, the latter fitted with single lug-sail and both fast and weatherly.

Still the small boats which continued to be built in the North Isles remained true to the sixareen model. This was not due to any prejudice against the "strangers'" boat, because quite a number of these were bought and used locally, but they did not quite suit local conditions and have now completely vanished. All that remains to mark the influence of the Scottish "invasion" is a moderate raising of the peak of the square-sail, making it more lug shaped, and more weatherly. Nor does it seem that the Dutch who came to Lerwick in such great numbers about the middle of the seventeenth century made any impression on the model of the Shetland boat. This might of course be accounted for by the fact that at that time the boats in use were mostly Norwegian-built.

It may be argued from the above that it was pure chance that Shetland has retained the early Norse model with so little change, the Dutch influence coming too early, and the Swedish and Scotch too late.

But it is much more probable that the suitability of these early boats for the purpose was the main reason for the survival of the model in true and unaltered form over so many centuries, and there is much evidence to show that this theory is the correct one.

Hardanger Boat with Shetland Square-sail.

The appearance of a small "cousin" from the west coast of Norway, for example, is hailed with delight. She is obviously of the same lineage, and immediately adopted into the fleet of small craft. She is similar to handle under oars or sail; is light and handy on a beach, and her lines are beautiful. There are several of these in the North Isles alone, but you will search in vain for a single small row or sail boat of Scottish build or type. Of course this does not apply to the larger decked motor fishing boats. In this field the fine new Scottish boats have almost completely ousted the Shetland model.

When the motor was first introduced for fishing boats some were installed in sixareen models and other motor boats were brought in from the Moray Firth coasts. Asked about the comparative merits of the two new types of line fishing boat, an experienced fisherman was rather non-committal, remarking that the Shetland boat was dryer but the Moray Firth boat a better platform. Today both types have been largely replaced by the fine dual purpose motor boats which are being built round the Scottish coasts and in Shetland as well.

For thousands of years before the advent of the long-ships of the Norsemen, man had been conducting a war against the sea. His weapons were timber, man power, and later the wind. By the time that the Oseberg ship was built there was not much he had to learn about the lines and construction most suitable for defeating the sea by timber and man power. He also knew something about enlisting the wind on his side by the use of sail, though in this direction great strides were still to be made.

The sixareen had the same sea to defeat by exactly the same means, namely, timber and man power with some help from the wind so that no great alteration in form of lines was to be expected.

It may seem strange that for so many centuries boats for use in Shetland continued to be built or fashioned in Norway. The proximity of, and ready access to that country is probably one of the reasons; affinity of language and racial ties another, and dislike of the early Scottish overlords who settled in castles at Scalloway and Muness and their tyrannous rule a third reason. But probably the most important reason of all was simply that the Norway boats suited the Shetland fishing better than any other type.

There was much in common between the boats of north-west Norway and the sixareen. They also used the square-sail, though on long passages, such as going north to the Lofoten fishing, they sometimes set a topsail over it, a thing not seen in Shetland. They too had a crew of six men and rowed when actually working lines, and depended on their sail for safety in scudding before the gale when caught out.

At the Lofoten fishing the men lived ashore in bothies as in Shetland, and when the fishing season was over the boats were sailed home and hauled out. Altogether, the method of fishing was so similar that boats built for the one would be suitable for the other also.

In Shetland the haaf-boat, or sixareen, stations were chosen for their proximity to the fishing grounds and suitable drying beaches, and as the fish were all sun-dried this was important—so important that where the choice lay between a secure anchorage for the boats and a good drying beach, the latter might be preferred, even though it meant that the boats had to be hauled out over the "helly" or week-end, or even after a single trip. These trips might last a couple or three days, after which six men might have to pull this 30 foot boat out of the water without any assistance, so weight was of great importance and anything that could be was made removable. It was important also because a light boat was easier to row than a heavy one, and it was not at all uncommon for crews to race each other to the fishing grounds in calm weather. Even a little unnecessary weight would tell in a 20-mile race.

To meet these needs the sixareen had to be of light draught with good waterline length, but not too much waterline beam. But she had also to be able to bring home a catch of fish, perhaps in rough weather. So she had flared sides, and as she went down her carrying capacity increased. These flaring sides and raked stems also gave her a big reserve of buoyancy and helped to make her the seaworthy craft that she was.

But these requirements of speed under oars or sail and seaworthiness were very much the same as were required of her Viking ancestors. The sea on which they were to sail was the same, and both were fashioned to give maximum speed on this sea with a minimum of effort.

Perhaps the Ness Yole, though smaller, is even nearer to the long-ship than the sixareen, because, while she too needed speed, her journeys were of shorter duration and less carrying capacity was needed.

On this matter of ancestry it is also of interest that the small boats found in the fore part of the Gokstad ship were not only similar to the ship itself, and in form nearly related to the boats of north-west Norway, but that for rowing they were fitted wtih something very like the "kaeb" and "humlibaund" of the Shetland boat today. This arrangement, though almost universal throughout these islands, is not found elsewhere round the British coasts.

A close comparison of the Shetland boat of yesterday and today with her Viking ancestors is possible on account of the remarkable finds in Southern Norway in 1880 and in 1904, when the Gokstad and Oseberg ships were excavated.

They had been ship-graves in the realm of the Ynglinger kings and are believed to have been the burial place of a chief and a Queen respectively, both of the Ynglinger Line. Professor Brögger has advanced the theory that it was Queen Aase, grandmother of Harald Fairhair, who was buried in the Oseberg ship, and this gives it rather a special interest. Though the older of the two, the Oseberg ship was in particularly good condition. Both have, however, been restored as far as possible out of the original material, and are to be seen in the Viking Ship Hall at Bygdöy, on the west side of Oslo Fjord. The Oseberg ship was built in the early decades of the ninth century, A.D., all of oak and with a beautifully carved serpent stem. She is a very large double-ended clench built boat, built for use on coastal journeys and was specially low wooded. The oar holes show that she could be rowed by 30 men, fifteen oars to each side and one man to each oar. Her mast was stepped near amidships and could be lowered towards the stern, as in all Shetland square-sail boats.

The Gokstad ship is generally similar, but rather deeper, having been intended for open sea journeys.

It is probable that the two Shetland types which show purest descent from their Viking ancestors are the Ness yole of today and the North Isles sixareen of yesterday, but as the latter did have to carry a more variable load than the yole, her dimensional proportions differ more from these ancient ships than do those of the yole.

On a recent visit to Norway Dr. Manson sent me a post card showing one of the small boats from the Gokstad ship, and I immediately noticed a conspicuous groove along the upper inner edge of the strakes in way of the rooves which seemed familiar.

Hasting to Haraldswick I examined a number of boats drawn up in their noosts there and found that several had this feature in rudimentary form, though now it does not appear to serve any useful purpose: an interesting example of a once ornamental or useful feature in the art of boat building being handed down from father to son for, shall we say, about 40 generations.

Chapter III.

THE NESS YOLE

Her hearth is wide to every wind
That makes the white ash spin;
And tide and tide and 'tween the tides
Her sons go out and in;

Kipling.

WHEN Ployen, Amtmand and Commandant of the Faroe Islands, visited Shetland in 1839, their ship was met by small boats after rounding Sumburgh, and he remarks on their similarity to the boats of his own islands. They were rowed by three men, each pulling a pair of short oars, and were undoubtedly the craft now known as Ness yoles. The men sat on straw plaited mats laid on the thwarts and Ployen thought that this plan might with advantage be adopted in the Faroe Islands.

In 1880 Tudor visited Fair Isle and gives a good description of the boat in which he landed. She was of the type used for saith fishing round the island and was rowed by three men or sailed. He considered her very inadequate for the "furious tideways" round the island, but remarks that the fishermen refused to change to larger boats, considering that their own were more suitable for the purpose. This preference seems to be justified by the fact that though it is now 70 years since Tudor's visit, the same type of boat is still in use in Fair Isle and in the south of Shetland.

The saith fishing seems to have been largely confined to these districts, and was by handline and sinker. Three men rowed the boat as fast as possible through, or along the edge of the tide and one worked the line. The boat is long, narrow, and no other boat of so extreme a type is found elsewhere in Shetland.

The Fair Isle boat of 1880 was of 16 ft. keel, 22 ft. 9 ins. overall, and 6 ft. beam. Her depth at stem-head is given as 2 ft. 3 ins.;* at stern-post 2 ft. 1 in.;* and amidships 1 ft. 9 ins. The sail was a square-sail, and even today the fishermen of the island of Whalsay claim that for a small undecked fishing boat this rig is still unsurpassed. Truly this is a remarkable tribute to the rig coming as it does from fishermen who for two generations have been accustomed to large sailing smacks, ketches, or motor boats for the summer herring fishing, and to smaller, but still powerful, decked motor boats for the winter haddock fishing.

---

*It must be assumed that Tudor's figures for depth at stem-head and stern should read 3 ft. 3 ins. and 3 ft. 1 in. instead of 2 ft. 3 ins. and 2 ft. 1 in. respectively, or that he has measured the depth from top of keel fore and aft to covering board as he has clearly done in getting the depth amidships. Either of these two assumptions is satisfactory, but unless one or the other is made the dimensions given by him do not represent anything the writer could imagine ever having been used or built in Shetland. It would be quite unsuitable for a seaway.

The yoles, though built primarily for speed, had also to be seaworthy craft as they fished in dangerous waters among the treacherous tides and cross currents which are particularly marked at headlands dividing the Atlantic Ocean from the North Sea. This speed had often to be got by man-power alone, so the ratio of length to beam had to be large, and the draught small. Any unnecessary increase in draught would have reduced this speed by adding to the resistance of the boat through water, while unnecessary freeboard would have had the same effect through presenting a larger surface to the wind.

These considerations remained very much the same as in the days of the long-ships, so it is not surprising that the lines remained similar. At the same time it must be recognised that by comparison with a yole a vessel like the Oseberg ship was very much under-powered. A yole on a displacement of little over half a ton rowed three men; the Oseberg ship on a displacement which was probably about forty times as much rowed only ten times the number of men. But man-power by oar has the limitation that the length of the side of the vessel more or less governs the number of oarsmen. Perhaps this is one of the reasons why Olaf Tryggvisson, about 200 years later, had the famous "Long Serpent" built at Ladehammer on Trondhjem Fjord. Length seems to have been her one outstanding feature: at least twice that of the Oseberg ship; but this great length compared with that of her opponents seems to have been a disadvantage in battle, and it was from her that Olaf conducted his last gallant fight.

So too with the yoles. There was a limit of length-to-beam and depth-ratio beyond which it was unsafe to go, and that perfection of model was reached a long time ago seems to be proved by a comparison of Ness yoles of today, and the Fair Isle boat of 1880 described by Tudor.

	Two man yole of Sandwick	Fair Isle boat of 1880	"Rodesport" LK. 103 of Scatness
Overall length	20 ft. 0 ins.	22 ft. 9 ins.	22 ft. 6 ins.
Length of keel	14 ft. 0 ins.	16 ft. 0 ins.	16 ft. 0 ins.
Beam	5 ft. 2 ins.	6 ft. 0 ins.	5 ft. 7 ins.
Height to top of planking at stem	3 ft. 0 ins.	3 ft. 3 ins.*	3 ft. 6 ins.
Height to top of planking at stern	2 ft. 10 ins.	3 ft. 1 ins.*	3 ft 1½ins.
Height to top of planking amidships	2 ft. 2 ins.	2 ft. 2 ins.†	2 ft. 2 ins.

An old yawl at Spiggie, probably built about the beginning of this century, was 23 ft. overall and 5ft. 9ins. beam. She had wooden "kaebs" instead of iron ones, and the wales were full length. In other respects she was almost identical with LK. 103 above.

As in all Shetland boats the stems are cross scharphed to the keel, the same method as was used in the Oseberg ship. There were six strakes a side in the two boats measured, and the wales tapered away finely and ended completely 18 ins. from the stems both fore and aft. This practice is to be seen in some of the smaller Norwegian skiffs, but not in the normal Shetland model boat, nor in all the yoles.

---

*See note on previous page.

†Tudor gives 1 ft. 9 ins. depth amidships and I have added the 5ins. of keel to make the figures comparable.

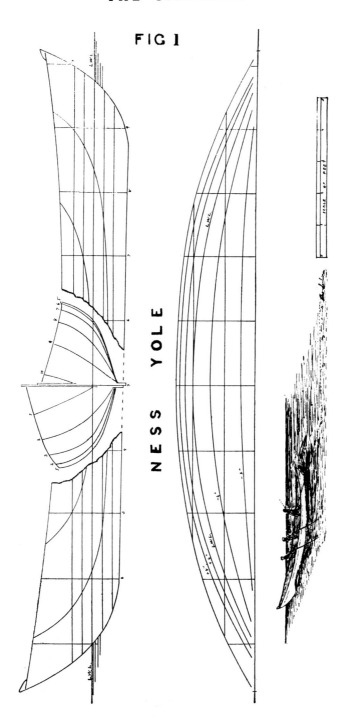

FIG 1

NESS YOLE

It doubtless aims at giving the boat flexibility, which is here usually associated with speed. Another difference is that the keel is slightly T-shaped, with garboards rising only about 24 degrees.

On this matter of flexibility: many years ago there was a story current here of a merchant vessel being chased and overtaken by a privateer, till her captain went below and cut all the hanging knees in the vessel. This done she escaped, but arrived in port, it is said, like a basket!

The two-man yole has two main timbers only, the three-man yole three, in each case spaced 3 ft. centres, and as the thwarts fit over these it means that the weight of the oarsmen is concentrated amidships to keep her lively in a seaway. Each man pulls a pair of 10 ft. oars, and the square-sail is still used.

Apart from general similarity of form, a close study of these craft brings out so many small points of resemblance to similar boats in Norway that there can be no doubt at all as to the common ancestry. But what does seem most remarkable is that in spite of the intimate contact between fishermen and boat carpenters of Shetland and Scotland for the last 70 years, there is not a single feature in even the newer boats that could be attributed to Scottish practice, though as has already been mentioned, the larger fishing boats now built in Shetland owe almost all to Scottish influence.

The reason is clearly that a long period of development has so perfected this model for her particular work that no alteration in form has been possible for at least 70 years, possibly for ten times this period.

The yoles are perhaps the most interesting craft to be seen in Shetland today, and they are still being built. These with the small "sixareen model" boats still used for handline fishing and for the "eela" look like holding their own against all comers.

The "eela", by the way, is the fishing of the young saith by means of rod and fly, so that the saith, in one stage or another of its growth, although gastronomically unexciting, has done more to preserve the purity of the model than any other fish in the sea.

Ness Yole at Sandwick.

Chapter IV.

THE HAAF FISHING

. . . . the sea is without mercy and never forgives. Punishment for a mistake, or error of judgment is meted out in full on the spot.".— Muhlhauser in *The Cruise of the Amaryllis.*

THREE important types of fishing were carried out in three different sizes of boat, now known as the sixareen model.

The "eela" or fly fishing for young saith, was around the bays, rocks and skerries and over the "baas" or shoals, and for this the smallest size of boat was used. "Fivla", built by Robert Nicolson in 1911, was typical; 10 ft. 2ins. keel, 17 ft. 9 ins. over stems and 5 ft. 2 ins. beam. This boat is still in use.

Next came the inshore fishing, particularly for haddocks and saith. It was mainly a winter fishing at grounds within a few miles of the shore, and for this good, roomy boats measuring from 19 feet to about 23 feet in overall length were used, and were commonly known as "fourareens".

Finally there was the "haaf", or deep sea fishing, on the more distant banks for cod and ling. This was essentially a spring and summer fishing and for it the sixareens were used. Not only was the distance greater, but the weight of these large fish much more than that of either of the other fishings and the boats might be at sea for several days in fine weather with the land quite out of sight.

The disastrous storm of July 1881, in which ten of these boats were lost, focussed attention on these light open boats that fished anything up to forty miles from the land and even occasionally farther. It has even been said that the fishermen of Shetland have been known to haul their lines within sight of the fishermen of Norway.

A good deal is known about this storm because it was possible to get first-hand accounts from men who had experienced it, both at sea and on the land.

The day was fine, almost calm, but there was a considerable swell in the Atlantic. The boats from Unst, Yell and Northmavine were fishing out to the north-west, on the edge of the continental shelf, where the sea bed drops within a couple of miles from 100 to 200 fathoms, and a few miles further right down to 600 fathoms. In the late afternoon cloud appeared in the north and a scurry of wind came down on the water, but lifted quickly. Then at about 5 p.m. a dark line appeared on the water and within a matter of minutes the wind struck the boats with such fury that many turned side on, the two oarsmen being unable to keep their bows up to the wind. At the same time the temperature fell sharply.

A North Isles man, who was a youth in one of the boats, admitted that he was frightened when the wind struck the boat, and as long as they were trying to get their lines. The sea got up almost at once, and a large barque appeared from the west and passed close by them as she scudded before the wind for shelter.

For a while they kept her head to wind, while they struggled with the lines, and with her buoyant bow and high sheer she kept wonderfully dry though the wind and sea were terrifying. Then the reefed square-sail was set and she was off like a race-horse for shelter, and his earlier qualms left him. Her skipper knew the dangerous tides off the north end of the island well and passed this about ten miles off, and so kept outside the strongest tides altogether till they were approaching Fetlar, where they cut through them and made Uyeasound.

It is said that most of the boats that failed to return were lost in attempting to approach the land through these fierce tidal streams, and in the semi-darkness caused by the storm and the naturally fading light of late evening.

A similar storm occurred in April 1927. It had been a day of light variable winds, with wandering showers, and mild for the season. At 5 p.m. one of these showers had just stopped when without warning the wind struck the building in which I was working, and at once it was blinding, driving snow. Within ten minutes all the five trawlers in the harbour were steaming to their anchors or had anchors up and were trying to make the pier. One got a glimpse of a moving vessel for a moment through the snow and then she was hidden again. By 8 p.m. it had moderated a little but was still intensely cold and snowing hard. The wind died away through the night and when daylight appeared there were two trawlers at the pier, and three beached in different parts of the harbour. Unable to make the pier and with anchors dragging they had steamed slowly ahead until the vessels grounded. The harbour being entirely sheltered they were undamaged.

It seems incredible that a 30 ft. open boat could live at sea in such weather, and yet this must have been like the storm of 1881, in which some of them even made record passages.

The Lofoten sea is subject to similar storms, and when the fishing was in open boats like those in Shetland the method of handling was also similar: running free in their native element, with the closest harmony of working between skipper and sailman. They too were very particular to get perfect balance between boat and sail, and in the trim of the boat herself. The skipper could tell by her "feel" if the boat was quite happy; and if not she would be much less safe.

The test of sea-going qualities of a boat is not so much that of survival—a barrel can do that—but of ability to continue her normal function, or journey. The more nearly she can do this the better her claim to seaworthiness.

The generally accepted principle for small craft in rough weather is that they should ride to a sea anchor, or that if over 40 ft. or so waterline they will be safe hove to. That great seaman, Voss, stresses the importance of doing this in good time before the seas get dangerous, or if one has run too long, then to take the sails down, still running, round up slowly, and set riding sail. He also points out that a vessel making a square drift with wind and sea is comparatively safe; a fact that is perhaps less commonly known than it should be.

But in this case the boat ceases to be a means of progression across the waters, and becomes an almost stationary stronghold against the fury of the sea. No more.

The claim that the sixareen was the finest craft ever devised for sheer seaworthiness is based on the fact that they could, and did, actually travel at almost incredible speeds in conditions when any other open craft of this size would be incapable of voluntary movement.

In highly competent hands the sixareen seems even to have been more at home moving through the sea than when riding to her lines or dodging head-on under oars.

An excellent first-hand account of the experience of one of these boats in the same storm of July 1881 was published in Manson's Shetland Almanac and Directory for 1932, written by the late Chas. Johnson, Toam, North Roe.

Charles Johnson was doing his first year in an off-shore boat. They were fishing from Uyea, Northmavine, and pulled "west and off" till they got the Ossa through marks in Heylor land. He says that these marks, with the compass, led them out a N.W., and that they went off-shore about 30 miles. They rowed for nine hours in a smooth sea, and from Uyea Isle would have covered 34 sea miles. This gives a speed of 3.8 knots, under oars, and assuming her to be one of the largest size sixareens of about 28 ft. waterline, this would be a very economical speed to move at.

The Ossa Skerry itself would disappear at 17 miles, so that they must have steered almost half the way by compass.

It is very difficult now to get properly authenticated records of the speed of these boats, but in this case the narrator was quite sure of the time they took to run in, and the point of arrival is also known with certainty, so that if their seaward position can be established the speed of the boat on the homeward journey will be known.

But before this let us note what the narrator has to say about this particular storm and something of their passage back to land.

He says that on reaching the grounds they shot six lines N.W. by N., and that these would stretch close on six miles, and that their outmost buoy was streamed in 96 fathoms. Then they hailed three lines to their mid-buoy and got 180 ling and some other fish. The weather was still fine and "nothing to show otherwise", but after commencing to shoot these wet lines N.N.E., a bat of wind came from the north with a little rain. It passed away and the sea fell flat. Soon after, however, they "heard and saw the weather coming". It struck them on the bow, and the boat paid off, and the sea commenced to rain over them. They could not manage the boat under oars to haul any more lines . Nevertheless on reaching their mid buoy they lifted this, and the fish on the line reaching out to seaward floated the line to the surface, but they already had about 26 cwt. and did not want any more as the boat was then in good trim. Then they set the close-reefed sail, put the tack forward (to allow them to reach) and two men took the halyards. Even before they set the sail she was "foaming at the bows under the bare mast".

The line had been cut at 9.30 p.m., before they set the sail, and the wind was then N. by E. With the general direction of their course towards shore this would have brought the wind three points abaft the beam, but as they often had to bear away and "run the seas" she must have had the wind broad on the beam at times.

They tried to avoid the heaviest of the breaking crests but once had to run it right in the centre: "This sea rose very high astern. They pressed her with the sail when the surge came around her, and although the sail was laid down she run in it for a bit (like a field of snow) and took water over both sides". This is quoted, as it shows how they used the sail, and the importance of having absolutely reliable men at the halyards or "tows". There were seven men in this boat, but only three were engaged in managing her: the skipper, who sat down to lee with the helm over his shoulder, and the tows-men. After starting they did not speak to each other. Each knew exactly what to do at any given moment and they worked as one man.

Even when reaching she was given more or less sail as circumstances required to avoid the worst of the breaking crests. Once when reaching she was caught by the "tail" of a breaking sea which smothered her from the mast aft, but still she sailed on.

At last they made Ronas Voe and ran in behind the Blade of Heylor: " We seen there were a lot of boats there; we came in-about and tied up; we got out; the skipper having a watch told us it was 1.30 a.m.—four hours running in".

Let us now try to fix the position of their lines on this particular day as accurately as possible on chart 2182c of 1929. It will have been noticed that the wind direction, and that of setting lines, is given to the nearest point of the compass, and as all fishermen are very particular about fixing the position where they get good catches, it will be taken that this was exactly as stated, namely 30 miles offshore and N.W. of the Ossa. But in 1881 there would have been one point more westerly variation of the compass, so the direction on the above chart must be set off N.W. by W. Adding six miles for the length of their lines we are just a fraction of a mile inside the 100 fathom line shown on the chart. The depth at this buoy was given as 96 fathoms.

A little further to seaward the chart shows 180 fathoms, while at 10 miles it has dropped to over 600 fathoms, so that the position in which they shot their lines was, to use unnautical language, just "on the brow of the hill", and the place most favoured by line fishermen.

This all fits together, so their mid-buoy will be assumed to have been in Lat. 60 degrees 43 minutes north, Long. 2 degrees 38 minutes west. That gave them a run of 37 sea miles to the Blade of Heylor, and an average speed over the whole distance of 9¼ knots. Incredible? Yes, but how can we escape reaching this conclusion? The narrator was sure about the time. He was not sure about the distance, but we have been at some pains to translate his statements into an actual position on the chart, and there, at the distance he gives, we get the depth he gives. He was a sailor as well as a fisherman and it is most unlikely that he would have used statute miles instead of nautical. But if he did, then their outer buoy would have been in 80, not 96 fathoms. He certainly could not have made that error. Depth is of great importance to a fisherman,

This speed is 30% greater than the critical speed* of a boat of 28 ft. waterline, and it will be shown in a later chapter dealing particularly with speed that this is by no means impossible for a boat of this type in sheltered water. But a boat that can put up such a performance as this in such a sea is surely one of the finest craft that man has ever contrived to build.

There is no reason to think that this was an isolated case. There were many sixareens at sea that day, and others may well have put up similar performances, but it just happens that in this particular case there was sufficient information to determine the fishing position with reasonable certainty, and the time had been carefully noted.

Before going on to a description of the boat herself, a few remarks as to their handling must be given.

Sometimes a sixareen was said to become "sea-loose", implying the conditions in which she was travelling so fast that the "fluid" under her became a mixture of air and water, and the noise made was said to be as if "she were being drawn through a beach of pebbles". When the sail was reduced she would become normal again.

Many sixareens had a row of reef-points running from the heel of the yard to a point in the leach somewhere below the peak cringle. This was the second reef to be taken in when running and made the sail more nearly square. The yard was attached to the fore side of the mast by means of a smooth, semi-circular piece of hardwood, called the "rackie", that would slide easily up and down. The single halyards or "tows" were attached to the yard between the arms of the rackie, and were passed through a sheave in the head of the mast. They were always endless, and attached to a large cleat on the after side of the mast at a convenient height, the fall leading up again to the yard.

As soon as it became rough the tows-man would take up his place on the thwart abaft the mast and facing forward, with this large cleat in front of him, and if the weather got worse you would see him take the turns off the cleat so as to be ready to lower or set at a moment's notice. This practice applies to all the square-sail boats, both large and small alike, but with the heavier gear of the sixareen in rough weather two men acted instead of one.

On either bow there were two or three holes for securing the tack of the sail. Close-hauled it would be further forward, and running, further aft.

When it was dark the tows-man kept one foot on the planking of the boat, and could tell by the feel of broken water beneath her when to lower the sail, and being a "lifting" sail it was not unduly heavy to raise or lower while the boat was sailing. If lowered right down it lay across the boat in front of mast and shrouds.

In tacking the sail was lowered and one side of the rackie untied. The yard was then drawn forward and turned and the clew passed round to the other side, while at the same time the tack would be taken to the other bow. The rackie was then refastened and the sail ready to set.

---

*Critical speed in knots = 1.34 √L.W.L.: for 28 ft. L.W.L. = 7.1 knots.

It is fifty years since the last of the North Isles sixareens was built, but the square-sail can still be seen on many of the smaller fishing boats. Though not quite so simple to rig or handle as the dipping lug of Scotland, it is a better sail for running. On the other hand the lug with its tight luff is a more weatherly sail.

The tendency in Shetland during recent years has been to retain the midship position of the true square-sail mast, but to raise the peak of the sail and so to get a tighter luff and a more weatherly boat. This is one of the results that racing has had on the smaller fishing boats, which, fishing near the land, have no need of a sail surpassing excellence for running.

With the haaf-boats it was quite different. Given their freedom, and deep water, they were comparatively safe, and this was more important than to be able to beat up quickly to the land against an offshore wind.

For hundreds of years up to the middle of last century the haaf fishing was the most important one in Shetland, and the sixareens were built and developed specially for this.

The haaf stations themselves were situated all round the islands so that many of the boats were fishing quite near the homes of the men. Each man provided his quota of lines, called a "packie", and made up of about 20 "boughts" of 40 fathoms each. At four fathom intervals along the line there were one fathom "tomes" with a single large ling hook at the end of each, and so a "fleet" of lines for a six-man boat would have about 1200 hooks.

Sixareens at Feideland, 1890.

Herring was the best bait, but if not obtainable conger or other fish was used. Once at the grounds it would take a couple of hours to set the line, and after "tiding" it for a couple of hours they would commence to "hail" This might take three or four hours depending on weather conditions and the number of fish, so that working one of these lines would take the greater part of the day. Thirty cwt. of fish would be a good catch, and at that rate a couple of "hails" would give the boat as much as she could carry in fine weather.

If the catch was heavy the stone ballast would be jettisoned as it could easily be replaced from the beaches ashore.

Like sailors the world over there were superstitions and taboos. The good-wife must not sweep out the house before her man left, or his good luck would go. Ballast stones with white streaks were looked on with disfavour. They would mean white water over the boat. A knife must not be stuck in the mast because the wind that this action would bring would be far too strong.

Many years ago, becalmed with a heavy boatload of salt in barrels, an old haaf fisherman looked across at me as we toiled at the oars, and taking out his knife with a conspiratorial smile, made as though to stick it in the fore side of the mast where the skipper would not see it!

Then he told this yarn. He was sailing in a big herring lugger, but the wind was so light that they could not get to sea. Someone, out of mischief, stuck a knife in the mast, and soon the wind began to come and they to move seaward. This was what all wanted, but the wind kept on coming and an hour later had got so strong that the trip had to be abandoned. They lowered the great lug sail and had to tie in five reefs before running back to the harbour which they had left only an hour earlier. With the wind came snow, and he said that they snowballed each other on the deck as they ran in.

He told me too of the races that they had to the haaf when he was a young man. Boat against boat for 20 miles, "kemping" he called it, and said that at the end there would not be a dry "stick" on their bodies, but if they beat old Geordie they would all be happy. Geordie was not easy to beat. He had had his boat built out of specially light larch with just such races in mind! And so the good natured rivalry which is so marked in the sailing races of these islands today was born in the sixareens of the eighties.

Chapter V.

THE SIXAREEN

"There is something wonderful about a ship . . . . .
Wood and iron and hemp—and yet, somehow, a soul".
A. S. Hildebrande in *Blue Water.*

THE word sixareen brings to mind a boat called "Spinnoway", acquired many years ago for the princely sum of £6. She had been built in 1889 and was then nearly a quarter of a century old, but built of oak and Scottish larch was still "tight, staunch and strong", and with a second-hand 7 horse-power engine costing £17 installed was to give many more years of good service.

Her first job as a motor vessel was to ferry barrels of blubber from the very last school of Uyeasound, or Caaing, whales which had been driven ashore.

These whales used to visit Uyeasound almost yearly, and so regular were these visits that people in the south end of the island used to keep their ponies tethered during August to be ready to dash off at the first cry of "whales". Every boat in the place was manned and a semi-circle made round the whales, gradually driving them towards the wide sweep of the white beach, and once the leader was stranded the others made little effort to escape.

It is said that it was not usual to drive them on a Sunday, and that one year when this was done the result was disastrous. The sailing ship which was to pick up the valuable cargo of blubber was long delayed on her way north by contrary winds, and again on her return journey. Finally she put into Stornoway and the crew left her reporting that the cargo had gone bad, and that the maggots had got to the mastheads!

In our case, however, everything went well, and the motor sixareen made several trips along the coast loaded with barrels of blubber and with a whale towing from each bow and one from each quarter. The tail was raised well out of the water and lashed to the wooden bit-heads. Thus two came to lie alongside and two behind the boat. They were not very large whales, about 20 feet long, and those alongside towed well but those on the quarters became difficult when there was the least swell. They would ride forward till it looked as if the whole thing meant to come aboard and then move back with a jerk nearly pulling the quarter posts out of the boat. It was quite uncanny the way those tails moved!

Soon after this the sixareen made a trip to an outlying group of islands, and the war of 1914/1918 having started, was reported as a suspicious craft. This caused considerable local excitement and resulted in a ban being placed on the use of motor and of sail. She returned to her home port quite unconscious of the hornet's nest she had raised, and set off again on a hunt for the lifeboats of a torpedoed vessel.

But again she got little credit, misreading the life-boats' signals and reporting the hostile submarine instead of towing the life-boats triumphantly back to port!

Later she went on Admiralty service for the remainder of the war.

The return of peace saw her making coastal passages with cargo, taking picnic and regatta parties from island to island, and even at her old job of working "great-lines", but now along the shores with an amateur crew.

Then for several years she ran a regular ferry service between two of the islands, and was there caught in mid sound by the storm of 1927 which has already been described.

At the age of forty years she moved round to the Atlantic coast of the islands, and trace of her has now been lost.

It is now 61 years since she was built—almost, but not quite, the last of the fishing sixareens to be built in this island. Members of her fishing crew said she was built specially with a view to better windward sailing, and that while she was certainly good in this respect she was not quite as good running in rough water as some of the other boats.

She was built by Robert Nicolson, the best known of all the North Isles boat builders, and at least one of whose smaller boats still takes a good place in the racing fixtures of the islands.

The sixareens were built as light as possible and their life as haaf boats was reckoned to be no more than seven years. The stress to which the boats might be put at any time made it imperative that everything about them was of the best and in perfect condition. But after their life as haaf boats was over there was often work of a less exacting nature that they could carry on for many times as long. The "Spinnoway" above is no isolated example.

For many years Scottish larch has been the wood most favoured for planking all Shetland boats, but Tudor describes the boats of 1878 as usually built of Norway pine, or occasionally with larch for the lower timbers and boards, so it may be that only the last of the sixareens were built of larch. Large trees free from knots were used, cut into planks of the required thickness just before use. In this state the wood was much more pliable than seasoned boards would have been and steaming was not required.

The boats were built by eye and foot-rule and the oak timbers put in after the boat was partly or completely planked up. They were all clench built, the fastening being hand-wrought iron nails. These nails were certainly rather clumsy and actually cost more than copper nails, but they did not stretch or draw out of the oak stems and timbers as copper was liable to do, and the old builders took no chances.

In examining many old boats I have never seen iron nails fail, but have seen several cases of sprung planking when copper has been used, both in Shetland boats and others.

Next in importance to an absolutely sound and resilient hull came the oars, kaebs and humlibaunds, and once these were made and fitted it was the responsibility of each man to see that his oar and fittings were always kept in good order.

The whole arrangements for rowing, though not seen elsewhere, are still the most popular for Shetland boats.   The inner end of the oar, up to the hand grip, is rectangular in section so that the oar cannot be feathered.   It rests on a piece of hardwood, the "ruth", which is often continuous over the whole length of side on which oars are used.   The oak kaeb is fitted through this and the gunwale and takes the forward thrust of the oar, while a cowhide thong, the "humlibaund", passing obliquely through the gunwale in front of the kaeb and round the oar limits its backward movement.   Thus the oar moves back against the thong after each stroke, and when accustomed to this idle movement it gives a pleasant rhythm to rowing.   While I like it less than the rowlock it does allow oars to be quickly and neatly brought aboard, still in their humlibaunds, and when the kaebs are lifted out, a clear full length gunwale.

The rudder too was of vital importance, and its mountings were of iron.   The lower one was a long hand forged pintle, attached to the rudder by a welded clasp, and entering a clasp loop on the sternpost a little below the waterline.

The upper mounting was of a novel type universally and exclusively used in Shetland.   It was designed to ensure easy shipment of the rudder at sea, and that once shipped it was quite secure.   Anyone who has tried to ship even a small rudder, with two equally long pintles, when the boat is moving will realize that it might be quite impossible with a large rudder in a rough sea.

With the Shetland plan attention could be concentrated on the lower mounting, and when the rudder was secure in its place there a loop on the fore edge of the rudder head was entered between two loops on the sternpost, and a bolt, kept in position by a third loop somewhat higher up the sternpost, was then slipped down through the loop in the rudder and the bottom loop, so that the rudder could not be lifted off and lost.

The loss of rudder in the small zulu boats of Scotland with their nicely raked sternposts and conventional rudder fittings is all too easy.   A touch on the bottom of the rudder when the boat is sailing fast and it is gone, and one is left with an idle helmpin and the prospect of manoeuvring with an oar over the stern until the rudder is recovered.   This very thing was experienced many years ago.   A rock had got out of place, or it may have been the presence of a fair person—long since become permanent sailing companion—led to an error in dead reckoning!   The deep heel of the zulu touched, and the rudder was gone.   It is only gratifying to remember that one was spared the final indignity of lowering the sail and resorting to a pair of oars!

Even the smaller decked herring fishing boats of Scotland used to unship the rudder when lying at nets, and to make shipping more easy a chain was attached to the top of the lower pintle on the sternpost and passed up through the lower rudder loop.

The method of handling the square-sail at sea and in rough weather has already been described.   It must however be stressed that the Shetland square-sail is quite different from the dipping lug of Scotland; quite differently rigged; and that it was universally used by the sixareens from Sumburgh to the Flugga, and from Foula to the Out Skerries.

A Sixareen of 1890.

Even today, and in spite of its more weatherly qualities, the dipping lug is not used, though standing lug and stemhead jib are common among the eela boats.

The mast of the sixareen was always stayed; the main shrouds were led well aft through a hole in the gunwale and up a couple of feet or so where it was secured to its own standing part by a shroud knot or midshipman's hitch. The forestay led through a hole in the stemhead or "horn" and was similarly fastened. This stay was vital as there was no band on the after side of the mastbox to keep the mast up when the sail was down. All East Coast luggers on the other hand had this band or a wooden "fid", and no forestay or shrouds.

The halliards or "tows" of the square-sail were always single, rove through a hole in the masthead and straight down to a cleat at a convenient height on the after side of the mast, and the fall commonly carried up to the yard again to form a downhaul. The "rackie" of the square-sail yard passed round the mast but was attached to the yard at both ends. In fact it belonged to the yard rather than to the mast.

All this is quite different from the lug rig where the traveller is permanently attached to the halliards, or tie, and permanently circles the mast and has the yard hooked on to it for raising. The halliards of the lug sail too are always set to the weather gunwale by means of a strong purchase.

Even the largest of the Scottish herring luggers were rigged this way. The foremast might be 60 ft. or 70 ft. long and 18 inches to 20 inches in diameter at the deck, and the halliards a huge tackle made up of two four sheave blocks, each almost as much as a man could lift. In these large boats the steam capstan was used to set the sail, to sheet it home, and of course to set the mast. Without it the crew could never have handled such heavy gear.

The lugger's mast was stepped well forward on a great oak block, and when lying at nets it was lowered, the heel leaving the step and sliding up the mast box till the mast rested on the breast beam and on a high crutch near the mizzen mast aft. Thus it was not fastened to the boat in any way.

North of Shetland a boat had the misfortune to lose her mast. It rolled overboard when being set in a heavy sea! It may be thought that this would end their sailing, but no, the crew of six set to, parbuckled it aboard somehow, and got it set.

This brings to mind the recent remark of a Shetland youth, when asked if he had found a certain job difficult. "It had to be easy", was his reply, "because it had to be done!"

But we are getting away from the sixareen. Her square-sail mast, unlike the luggers, was stepped amidships.

The model of a Foula boat of 1880 shows it at .53 of the boat's overall length from the fore side of the stem. Models of sixareens in the Town Hall, Lerwick, and the Public Hall, Baltasound, both show it at .45. The North Isles sixareen "Spinnoway" had the mast at .46, and the Ness Yole "Rodesport" of today has it at .51. It may be of interest to note here that in the Oseberg and Gokstad ships of the ninth century A.D. it was at .46 and .51 respectively.

Photographs of sixareens at Feideland about 1890 confirm this. Five of the six boats have their masts at .45, .46, .47, .48, .48 respectively. The sixth, 617 LK., has it at .38. That is to say one taft further forward. Does this reflect the influence of the East Coast lugger which had her mast somewhere about .25?

If so it can hardly have been a success as it was not repeated in the later boats or models mentioned above.

Attention is particularly directed to these points about rig and mast positions because they show that the proper and only place for a square-sail mast is still near amidships as it was in the old longships, and because I have seen an old woodcut that depicts a sixareen rigged without shrouds or forestay, and with halliards consisting of a tie and tackle to the weather gunwale: all features of the Scottish lug, but quite incorrect for a sixareen.

The sheet of the sixareen was an endless rope attached to the sail at one end, passing in through a hole (or bore) in the gunwale, and back through a thimble or small block in the clew of the sail, and was held by the steersman. This is exactly the same as described by Ployen in 1839. In Faroe they used the same lead but the sheet was held by a second man and the tows by a third, so that in Faroe the safety of the boat depended on mutual understanding and action by three men instead of on two, and Ployen thought that the Shetland method was the better one.

He also refers to the superiority of the Shetland multi-line bowline over the "bydevindsseilads", or single line bowline, used in Faroe, and describes it as a number of lines which are made fast to the "leach" from the yard down towards the tack of the sail, shorter as they approach the middle and united by a strong knot, and tightened by a line which worked on them all.

From this it is clear that the bowline was perfected in Shetland as early as 1839.

But now authorities differ as to how and where this single line should lead. Over the forestay to the lee side or "hinnie spot", or straight to the "horn"? From information I have been able to get locally (some dating from 1911) it should lead over the forestay, and this does seem the most effective lead for the purpose. On the other hand it is quite commonly shown leading straight to the stem. Perhaps practice in this matter differed from district to district.

The question arises: when did the haaf boat of Shetland become a distinct and independent model? That is to say a boat built in Shetland for this particular fishing, and native to the Islands in conception as well as in build.

A study of contemporary literature throws a good deal of light on this point. When Ployen visited Shetland in 1839 this new type had largely replaced the Norway yawls, for he says, "the ordinary fishing boats are of the size of eight-manned boats with us (Faroe), but considerably broader, and rowed by six men. These circumstances evidence that the Shetlanders use the sail more than the oars, and the sail itself indicates the same fact". He was studying the ling fishing particularly and visited Feideland where 40 boats were working, but makes no reference to any Norway yawls among the fleet, or any reference to the similarity of any of the boats fishing there to those at Faroe, though, as has already been mentioned, it was this very similarity of the three-man boats which they encountered after rounding Sumburgh Head that attracted his attention.

The haaf boats of 1839 were therefore of a different build from the Norway yawls.

But this was not the case in 1817 when Hibbert visited the same station. He calls the haaf boats "a fleet of yawls" and says that frames ready modelled and cut out in Norway were imported, and when put together formed a yawl of six oars from 18 to 19 ft. in the keel and 6 ft. beam.

He quotes Sherriff for the further particulars: 20 to 24 ft. from stem to stern, depth $2\frac{1}{4}$ to $2\frac{1}{2}$ ft. and sail $15\frac{1}{2}$ ft. deep by 12 ft. broad at top and 14 ft. at the foot. These are the proportions of a Norway yawl and not of a sixareen.

He describes his return from a visit to Foula, however, as being made in a "large boat sailing to Vailey from the Haaf". It is clear that this was an open boat as he speaks of her shipping much water, and she may have been a sixareen.

It is certain, therefore, that between the years 1817 and 1839 a new type of haaf-boat came into common use, and that for this fishing at least she had by the latter date largely replaced the boats from Norway.

Model of LK. 2615.

This is generally confirmed by Tudor (1878/1879), who states that up to 40 or 50 years earlier all the haaf-boats were imported from Norway in pieces ready for putting together.

That this import of boats had been very large is shown by figures of imports quoted by O'Dell: year 1806, "27 set up boats"; year 1820, "18 built boats and 21 in boards"; year 1829, "193 boats in boards and 50 in boards". All were from Bergen.

There is no doubt that the great disaster of 1832 would accelerate the replacement of the older type of haaf-boat by the larger and more able sixareen. An effort was even made to introduce half-decked boats, but the fishermen did not favour this.

On the evidence of the above facts the birth of the sixareen as an independent model may be placed somewhere in the early years of last century, with the strong probability that she did not assume a position of paramount importance till after 1832.

It is worth noting too, that while Tudor uses the word "sixareen", it is not used either by Ployen or by Hibbert, so probably had its origin after 1839, by which time a number of these boats must have been in use. It is given in Edmondston's Etymological Glossary of 1866.

One is led to speculate by what stages the sixareen model came to replace the Norway yawl in the smaller craft.

Doubtless the builders having obtained their freedom would experiment with variations in hull proportions, and also produce smaller models of the new type, and by degrees these would replace the older models wherever they were more suitable. The fourareens, for example, which were also required for working lines at sea, would quickly become the reduced versions of the successful sixareen model which they are today. For the smallest sizes, however, the whillies and the eela boats, the sixareen model has not been completely adopted, and looking at the scores of these little boats in the noosts today a considerable variety of shape is seen from miniature sixareens to something not very greatly different from the Ness yole.

That a great deal of experimental work was done even in the later years is proved by the rather amazing fact that as long as sixareens were being built in the North Isles individual boats were frequently altered after they were built. They would be taken back to the builder in the off season, and their behaviour discussed with him, with the result that the boat would be "laid out" over the fore "baund", or taken in at the after "stameron". Next season her performance would be again compared with that of neighbour boats.

This was surely full scale experiment of the most practical kind, and thus tested under oar and sail, in calm and in storm, the perfect model would gradually evolve.

There were many builders scattered throughout the islands, each separated from the other by considerable distances, and each developing his own particular model. And yet there do seem to be fairly definite limits to the proportions of a sixareen, arrived at independently by all these builders.

The difference between a good boat and an indifferent one lay rather in the fine modelling of the lines, and it is important therefore to judge the model by the best examples.

Fortunately full details of several boats by well known builders have been preserved.

Chapter VI .

THE SIXAREEN — DIMENSIONS AND LINES

"Build me straight, O worthy Master!
Staunch and strong, a goodly vessel,
That shall laugh at all disaster,
And with wave and whirlind wrestle!"

Longfellow.

OF the fine fleet of fishing sixareens that existed in Shetland towards the, end of last century not one is left. A few fourareens, boats of about 21 ft. to 22 ft. in overall length, are still to be seen in the "noosts", at rowing contests in local regattas, and occasionally fishing, but although of similar model they never enjoyed the fame of the sixareens.

Throughout the Islands, also, there are great numbers of eela and other small fishing boats, also of sixareen type. Many of these small boats are being fitted with, or built specially for motors, without modification of shape, and this is surely a high compliment to the perfection of the model.

In the south of Shetland and Fair Isle both this type and the Ness yawl, or yole, are to be seen, and the latter forms the connecting link with the old Norway yawl.

In Norway too development has been along similar lines to that in Shetland and some of the small open boats built on the Hardanger Fjord approach the sixareen fairly closely in general proportions.

It is fortunate that we have full dimensions and lines, or models, of several sixareens, and these show the proportions that were used by one or two of the best known builders in the Islands, and how near to each other these were.

There are available for study the lines drawings of two sixareens; "Old Times" of Lerwick, and "Spinnoway" of Haraldswick. Both these boats were by very well known builders.

There are also three models of sixareens; one by David Henry of Foula in 1880, one by John Shewan of Lerwick about 1910, and one by Magnus Johnston in 1925, so that we have Shetland pretty well covered.

The model by Magnus Johnston does not represent any particular sixareen, but rather a typical North Isles boat of the end of last century. He was a keen racing skipper, and an expert small boat and model maker, and apart from his own observation and measurements of many sixareens, he checked up every detail with old sixareen men to make sure that the model should represent the best North Isles practices. So beautiful indeed are his models, and so great was his genius as a designer, that I have sometimes wondered whether a sixareen built to his model, incorporating the best features of many good boats, would not herself surpass any one of them.

For comparison the table appended includes along with the sixareens a Hardanger built boat, a Ness yole, and the Oseberg ship of the ninth century.

The boats and models differ greatly in size and scale, so to make comparison more easy they have all been reduced to a common overall length of 30 ft.: that is, to the average length of a fishing sixareen.

No. 2 of the Table, a Ness yole of today, has less height and beam than any of the other boats, and so makes a connecting link between them and the ancient Oseberg ship.

No. 3 of the Table, a Norway boat of 1934, approaches quite near to the sixareens in all except draught.

But perhaps the most remarkable thing shown by the table is the striking similarity between the "Hope" built by John Shewan in Lerwick in 1910, and the "Spinnoway" built by Robert Nicolson in Haraldswick in 1889. The "Hope" was a larger boat, but reduced to the same size; the only difference between the two is that "Hope" has slightly less sheer, resulting in 2 inches more midship depth, and 2 inches more beam.

These boats were built at almost the opposite ends of Shetland, and separated in time by an interval of 20 years, and yet the final dimensions reached by each builder are almost identical!

The "Old Times" has flatter garboards and less depth in consequence, and a few inches more beam, but apart from this she differs little from the other two.

No. 4 of the Table is a Foula boat of 1880. Her beam is much greater than any of the other boats and her stems are of a different shape: more raked, and straight for the lower two-thirds of their length, and then curved upwards, thus comparing more nearly with the small boats of Sweden which visited Shetland in numbers at the end of last century, than with sixareens of the Mainland and North Isles of Shetland. I think it must be assumed that this model reflects a slightly different line of descent.

The model, however, conforms to the usual Shetland practice in respect of rigging, tows, rackie, and the cleat on the after side of the mast, proving that the method of handling the sail was identical. The oars, kaebs, humlibaunds, and rudder mountings are also identical with the rest of Shetland.

In the lines of "Spinnoway" the fore and aft under-water sections are very similar, giving what looks a rather full displacement curve forward. This is quite typical of these boats, and with their hollow mid-sections and straight keels it cannot be otherwise.

Sixareen men have told me that the powerful shoulders and roomy forehead of these boats was to guard against the danger of being "run under" by shipped water rushing forward when she plunged in a following sea.

Her displacement in fishing trim would have been about 3 tons, but in order to make the boats as light as possible for handling on a beach and for racing under oars to the haaf everything that could be made removable was made so. All the tafts, except mid and pump, could be removed, and reduced to a bare hull she would weigh no more than 16 cwt.*

As in the days of which the Sagas tell, whale ribs were much valued as "lins" to slide the boats up and down the beaches. They are remarkably slippery when wet and have the further advantage over wood that they are just heavy enough to sink in water, and so to stay put while the boat is got in position.

Although more difficult to come by now than formerly, some of these will still be seen in the noosts around the shores.

Feideland was one of the best known fishing stations, and when Ployen visited it in 1839 there were 40 sixareens fishing there. It has a tiny curved bay of light shingle, sheltered by a high green and rocky headland at the extreme north point of the Shetland mainland, and not easily accessible except by sea.

Photographs show some of the fishermen's bothies in the background with boats drawn up on the beach as well as a number of the large rectangular fish vats in which the split fish were salted.

But most interesting in these photographs are the sixareens themselves, afloat and in fishing rig, and perhaps they are the only ones of this date (1890) in existence. The rigging of the boats can be seen clearly, and the white square-sails stowed forward and over the bows. One is moored to a pigskin buoy and has her oars run forward and inboard but with the blades projecting overside. Another is seen with crew aboard just setting off for the fishing.

The photos are the property of Mr J. D. Ratter of Lerwick, and were taken by him when a boy.

The photograph of LK. 2615 reproduced on page 28 is from a beautiful rigged model in the Royal Scottish Museum. It shows the details of hull construction and of rigging in great detail even to the tying of the rackie, the typical sixareen box pump with tunnel delivery over the after taft, and the standard pattern of rudder mountings which have already been described at length.

It is right that details of these craft should be carefully preserved, because in their day they represented man's most perfect effort to produce a craft light enough to be handled afloat or ashore by six men, yet large enough to bring home a good burden of fish; a craft that would be light to row, and under sail respond instantly to control; a craft, in fact, that would give confidence to men whose livelihood had to be won in dangerous waters.

---

*Three-quarter inch planking 850 lbs. Oak, elm or redwood, keel, stems, timbers, wales, haddabaunds, wearings, tafts, fiskafel, 600 lbs. Iron fastenings, tar, pump, etc., 300 lbs. Total 1770 lbs.

The New Sixareen.

One can imagine the critical eye which a skipper would focus on a new boat before she left the builder's shed, and how, with his long experience he would picture her behaviour under different conditions of sea.

She must be light for rowing and pulling up the steep beaches, but resilient and strong, as the safety of her crew depended on this, and on the sweetness of her lines.   So between fisherman and builder the perfect form would gradually be developed.

(The New Sixareen)

The skipper sucked his pipe stem
 As he looked the new boat o'er,
And he saw her afloat on the ocean
 Full forty miles from the shore.

The skyline hard and dark,
 And the sea all flecked with white,
Where the taut line stretched to windward
 In the quickly failing light.

The "shott" was full of fish,
 And the boat rode deep in the sea:
While dark clouds loomed to leeward,
 Away where the land must be.

And he saw her pressing homeward
 In a smother of foam and spray,
Where the great Atlantic combers
 Spilled their crests along her way.

He turned his eyes to her quarters,
 And forward along her side,
And noted the powerful shoulders
 That the threatening seas would ride;

The sheer of the tough larch planking,
 The "timmers" and "hadda-baunds",
And he looked at the "tafts" and the "stameron",
 And withdrew a "kaeb" with hand . . . .

Then he took his pipe from his mouth,
 And filling it full anew,
He turned to the builder man
 And he said to him—"She'll do".

COMPARISON OF SIXAREENS AND SOME OTHER CRAFT.
(All dimensions reduced to 30 feet overall length.)

	Viking Ship	Other Craft		Sixareen Models			Sixareens	
	1	Ness Yole 2	Norway Boat 3	Foula Model 4	Lerwick Model 5	Baltasound Model 6	"Old Times" 7	"Spinnoway" 8
LENGTH O.A.	30' 0"	30' 0"	30' 0"	30' 0"	30' 0"	30' 0"	30' 0"	30' 0"
L.W.L.	—	24' 6"	26' 0"	—	26' 9"	—	26' 5"	26' 9"
Keel	—	20' 0"	17' 8"	17' 9"	—	—	19' 6"	19' 6"
HEIGHT Forward	2' 3"	4' 8"	5' 3"	5' 8"	5' 9"	5' 10"	5' 5"	5' 9"
HEIGHT Amidships	—	2' 11"	3' 5"	4' 3"	4' 4"	—	3' 11"	4' 2"
HEIGHT Aft	—	4' 1"	4' 2"	5' 6"	5' 0"	5' 3"	4' 7"	5' 0"
FREEBOARD Forward	1' 2"	3' 4"	3' 10"	—	3' 6"	—	3' 7"	3' 8"
FREEBOARD Amidships	—	1' 5"	1' 9"	—	1' 10"	—	1' 10"	1' 10"
FREEBOARD Aft	—	2' 6"	3' 0"	—	2' 4"	—	2' 3"	2' 6"
DRAFT at mid l.w.l.	1' 1"	1' 6"	1' 8"	—	2' 6"	—	2' 1"	2' 4"
BEAM greatest	7' 3"	7' 5"	8' 3"	9' 6"	8' 3"	8' 6"	8' 6"	8' 1"
from stem	—	—	—	—	—	—	13' 3"	13' 6"
l.w.l. beam	5' 10"	5' 11"	6' 8"	—	—	—	7' 1"	7' 1"
MAST, length	—	—	—	21' 0"	23' 6"	23' 6"	23' 0"	22' 6"
from stem	—	—	—	14' 10"	—	13' 10"	—	13' 10"
YARD	13' 10"	15' 4"	—	10' 0"	15' 5"	14' 6"	15' 0"	13' 6"
Sail area in square ft.	—	—	—	150	—	230	—	270

No. 1 The Oseberg Ship of ninth century A.D., length 70½ feet.
No. 2 Ness Yole, "Roodesport" of Scatness, as used today, length 22½ feet.
No. 3 Norwegian three-plank boat, built on the Hardanger Fjord in 1934, length 17 feet.
No. 4 Model of Foula Boat, built by David Henry, of Foula in 1880, now in the Royal Scottish Museum, Edinburgh, length of model 69 inches.
No. 5 Model of sixareen "Hope" LK. 225, built by John Shewan of Lerwick in 1910, now in Lerwick Town Hall. Length of "Hope" 36 feet, length of model 36 inches.
No. 6 Model of a North Isles sixareen, built by Magnus Johnston in 1925 and now in the Public Hall, Baltasound. Length 30 inches.
No. 7 "Old Times", a sixareen of Lerwick, built by John Shewan, length 30½ feet. Dimensions from drawing by Arthur Johnston.
Dimensions from drawing made by author. Length 30 feet.
No. 8 "Spinnoway", a sixareen of Haraldswick. built by Robert Nicolson in 1889.

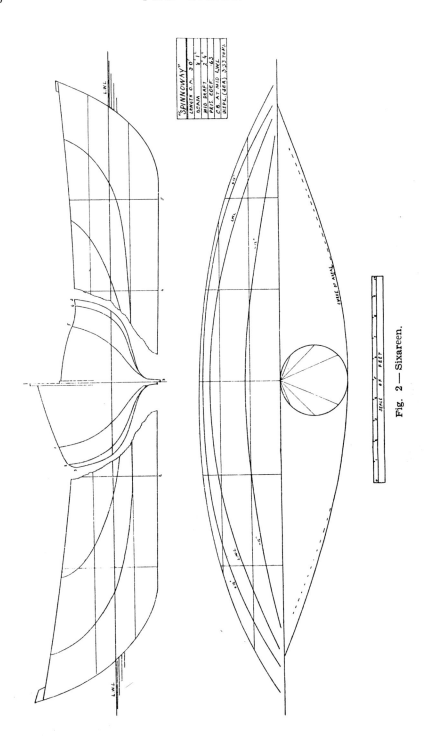

"SPINNOWAY"	
LENGTH O.A.	30'
BEAM	9' 1"
MID DRAFT	2' 4"
PRIS. COEF.	.63
C.B. AT MID LWL	
DISPL.(SEA)	3.33 TONS

Fig. 2 — Sixareen.

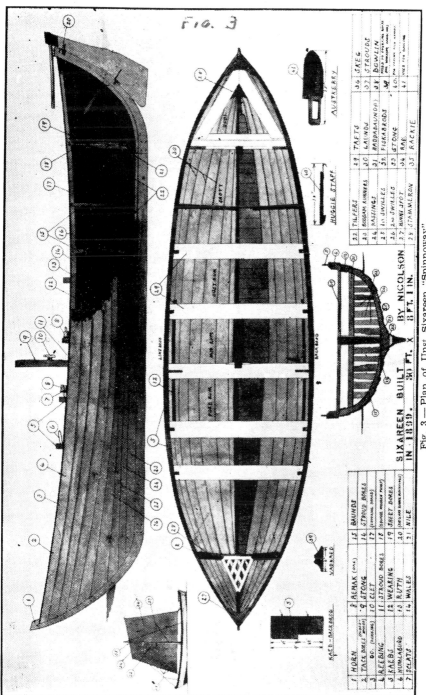

Fig. 3.—Plan of Unst Sixareen "Spinnoway".

Chapter VII.

THE SHETLAND RACING MODEL

"Three hundred pounds of timber, strong clenched with copper nails,
A good spruce mast from Norway, and Egyptian cotton sails.
All wrought and fashioned just so, by cunning craftsmen's hands,
With good Scotch larch for planking, and straight grained oak for bands".

THE fishermen of Shetland have always raced. "Kemping"* they called it in the North Isles, and still do.

Writing in 1809 Edmondston speaks of the rather unnecessary practice of boats from one station starting all together and racing the whole way to the fishing grounds. Old sixareen men have told me the same thing, boat racing against boat for four hours at a stretch, and under oars the whole way.

And so when racing started towards the end of last century the fishermen took to the sport like ducks to the water.

The boats were there too, and in the early races any model or rig was allowed, so that one could see fifies, zulus, ships' gigs, Orkney boats, and deep keel models all sailing together with the boats of Shetland. Some of the strangers had lead or iron keels, and were half decked, but the native craft were always in greatest numbers, and generally without decks or ballast keels.

The Unst Boating Club at once adopted the Y.R.A. rating rule of 1896, and this rule for linear rating, with a handicap of 15 seconds per foot per mile, is still in use. In fact it is now used throughout the North Isles of Shetland, except for square-sail and some of the smaller classes where the waterline alone is measured.

This rule was introduced by the Y.R.A. to replace the length and sail-area rule with its crushing tax on sail area, which had resulted in yachts of the day being terribly under-canvassed. On the whole the rule of 1896 has proved satisfactory in Shetland, though when the whole islands race under rules which either impose a very small tax on sails ($\frac{1}{2}\sqrt{\text{l.w.l.}}$) as in this rule, or no tax at all as in the case of waterline rating, large sails are to be expected. They run about 230 to 260 square feet per ton of displacement.

It may be thought that a shallow open boat without decks or ballast keel would be hopelessly outsailed by deep keeled half decked boats, but it did not work out quite like this, and the local models always took a fair share of the prizes in open races, and so, as there were always races confined to the undecked Shetland boat as well, the other craft tended to lose in popularity.

For these latter races ballast keels were not allowed, and the depth of keel below the garboards was limited to 6 inches. New boats being built for racing

*Norwegian, "kamp" equals fight or combat.

"Flying Cloud", 1950.

naturally conformed to these rules, as their owners would wish to compete in every possible race, and it was soon found that the best of these boats were quite as good as anything sailing in the open races.

Some years ago I read that a double-ended boat usually "sailed very slowly nowhere". A catchy phrase certainly, but I think well off the mark! In fact I believe that on the other hand the Shetland model with weighted keel is beginning to show superiority over other types in the model boat races held on some of the local lochs. Be this as it may she has certainly driven all other types off the sea in local regattas.

That is not to say that under certain conditions a different model may not show up well enough. A beamy and deep half-decked zulu, for example, which I sailed for several years both with standing lug, and with bermuda sail plan, did well enough in light winds, but was quite out of it in a blow. Although weatherly enough under hard weather conditions she was too short in the waterline for speed off the wind, and to win races in Shetland a boat must make speed on all points of sailing.

Spinnakers are not allowed, but in the North Isles jib-booms are attached to the mast by a goose-neck and are squared away when running. This saves cost in sails and the jib makes a passable substitute for the old type spinnaker and helps to balance the boat. The actual area of the sails is measured, so no restraint is imposed in the matter of rig, which is usually standing or sliding gunter lug and jib set flying on a rather long jib-boom to clear the mast. Recently I have tried a short jib-boom and genoa, and while this is nice to sail with the low cut of the sail itself obstructs vision on the lee bow (the most important lookout on the old sailing ships), and has the further disadvantage that to get full use of the sail in running the jib-boom must be extensible. This rather complicates the rigging in a small boat.

In Lerwick squaring jib-booms is not allowed, and there is a tendency to follow this lead in the North Isles on stormy days on the grounds of safety.

In this connection it has to be kept in mind that these boats will sink instantly if filled, and on a rough day with one of the crew bailing almost continuously the margin of safety is not very large and depends on the proper easing by helm and sheets, and where a race may be lost or won by seconds even an inch on the sheets may be grudged.

Sometimes the "oust room" of the boat is cleared of all obstructions and a curved sheet of metal fitted close to the planking from gunwale to gunwale. A long handled wooden shovel, operated by a man on the weather gunwale, is then used to keep the boat clear of water. It is a most efficient way of doing so, and credit for the idea goes to the island of Yell, though some hard worked member of the crew finding that he can hardly get his back straight next morning may disagree!

Most of the racing is done in the months of July and August when wind speeds are as a rule not very high.

Up to about 14 knots all the boats will carry full sail, but when the wind reaches 20 knots all will be reefed.

As the boats have to come considerable distances to these races postponement is not favoured and is a rather rare occurrence.

The 1950 races at Uyeasound were sailed in a rather rough day. Glass 29.4, wind S.W. and squally and something over 20 knots. This direction of wind knocks up a nasty short sea in West Sound where there are strong and uncertain eddy currents from Blumel Sound.

The course was the usual one and is shaped like a wide "A" of 4.7 miles, and twice round gives the full course a length of 9.4 sea miles.

The winning boat, "Miss Gadabout", sailed this course in 1 hour 56 minutes 0 seconds, and the second boat, "Laughing Water", in 2 hours 0 minutes 30 seconds.

The course involved a dead beat out the rough West Sound of 1.1 miles on each round, so that the total distance actually sailed by the boats (including the tacking) came to 10.3 sea miles and their average speed through the water for the whole course was 5.33 and 5.13† knots respectively.

That is to say the whole race was sailed at just about 96% of their respective critical speeds.

On the long free reach down Skuda Sound the smaller boat actually averaged 6.7 knots, or 25% over her critical speed, while on the run back, with the wind almost dead aft, the speed was 6.15 knots. In this race jib-booms were not squared away.

It was a fine sight to see these boats foaming in before the wind to the home mark, jibing over with precision, and tearing off down the Skuda reach in a scurry of white water with every stitch of canvas doing its job.

It is usual to arrange the sail-plan so that the boats carry just a touch of helm close-hauled. On a free reach or with the wind out on the quarter, however, they may carry some helm.

It has sometimes been suggested that in building these boats for racing they will lose some of their ancestral sea-worthiness, but I do not think that this is the case.

Again it must be said, of course, that it depends what one means by this expression. If this implies simple ability to live through any sea then we cannot beat the barrel or steel drum! But if it means to proceed on her journey under sail— and these boats are built for sailing—in foul weather as in fair, then I think that they are quite as seaworthy as their ancestors.

Actually they do not differ very greatly from these except that the ends are perhaps more carefully modelled, and this makes them extremely clean and safe in running.

Of course the high gunter rig is not ideal for open sea work in rough weather. The mainsail is extremely difficult to lower when running, or even to reef when the movement of one man to the mast may put the boat out of trim, and yet how else can the boat be eased?

In this connection it may be interesting to remark that these boats will claw to windward under jib alone in reasonably sheltered water. This was discovered more by accident than by design!

---

† All speeds are given in knots on basis of 6080 ft.

It is important to understand the behaviour of the Shetland boat when heeled, as it is on this that her safety and that of her crew depends.

The waterline beam is considerably less than that at the top of the sheer strake, and so she heels to one plank of freeboard—they are all clench built—quite quickly, unless she is being "sat up". From this point to gunwale awash she rapidly becomes stiffer, and in steady winds can be sailed with the water running along the covering board with perfect safety. The midship freeboard being rather low this will only mean a sailing angle of about 30 degrees, and the crew sitting up or out to windward adds very greatly to stability, and as long as nothing more than small wave tops are lopping aboard she is all right. But they must not be allowed to accumulate in the lee bilge, and this is where the shovel proves its usefulness.

Racing in squally weather, however, a length of the side may possibly go down. If this happens the inflow of water increases with alarming rapidity, and there is nothing for it but to let the sheets fly instantly otherwise she must fill and go down. This is nothing against the model, rather the reverse, as it implies that even when through bad seamanship the craft has been put in danger she will yet give one a better chance than by capsizing.

If not racing sail would probably have been reduced before this point was reached, but it is not possible to reef a gunter lug, or even to change a jib, in a close race and leave any hope of winning.

Nor will the race be won if it is necessary to stop frequently to bail the boat out, so she must be nursed through the squalls.

Although the boat must never be allowed to take more water than the "shovel man" can put back it is not necessary to keep one eye glued to the lee side. Far from it. An occasional glance to see that all is well is usually all that is required, for knowing the boat it will be possible to tell by the feel—the violence of a forward plunge, or upward acceleratiton of the weather gunwale on which you are probably sitting—that water is about to come aboard or the side go under. More, you may even estimate the quantity, and in that split second of time available decide whether she can take it, or whether, and to what extent she must be eased.

If close-hauled the helm can possibly do it, or helm with a few inches off the main sheet, leaving the jib to help her away quickly after the luff. But again much depends on the particular boat, her sail-plan and her crew. Some boats prefer the jib eased first. Everything must be just right and work in perfect harmony.

Fig. 4 has been prepared to give an idea of the performance of these boats. It shows the Uyeasound course and the track of the winning boat "Mareel", in one of the races in 1948. This boat is 17 ft. 2 ins. on the waterline, 5 ft. 10 ins. beam, and carries a sail-plan of 248 sq. ft.

In this race there was a fresh S.E. breeze and all boats carried full sail, and the course of 9.4 sea miles was sailed by the winner in 1 hour 59 minutes and 23 seconds.

There was a dead beat down Skuda Sound so that the race would be reckoned a fast one.

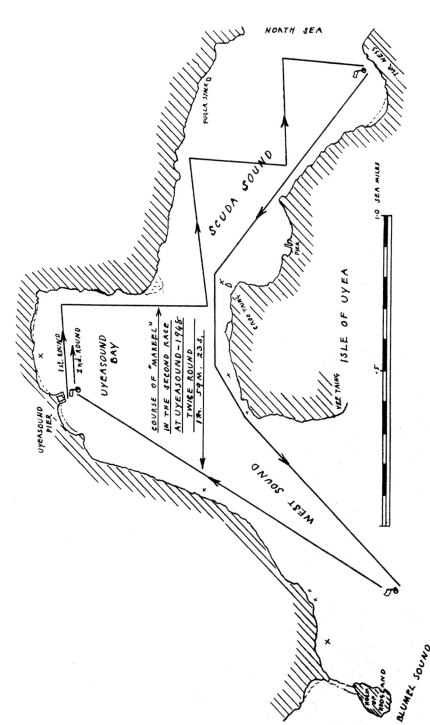

NORTH SEA

TAK NESS

FUGLA STACK

SCUDA SOUND

ISLE OF UYEA

PIER

CROO TAING

VER TAING

UYEASOUND
BAY

1st. ROUND

2nd. ROUND

UYEASOUND PIER

COURSE OF "MAREEL"
IN THE SECOND RACE
AT UYEASOUND—1948
TWICE ROUND
1 h. 59 m. 23 s.

WEST SOUND

1·0 SEA MILES

·5

BLUMEL SOUND

HUGA
OFFLAND
HOSSLAND

Fig. 4 — Regatta Course.

In this race "Mareel" was followed closely by an old rival "Miss Gadabout", also of 17 feet waterline, while third place was taken by the much smaller "Ruby". Now it is interesting to note that the winner was designed and built in Lerwick, the second in Fetlar, while the third was a fishing boat from the West Side of Shetland converted to a racer, and yet when handicaps were allowed there was under four minutes' difference between the three.

Over many years a good deal of attention has been given by builders all over Shetland to improving the sailing qualities of the model, but by and large the most successful boats do not differ very greatly from one another in general proportions, or for that matter in size. With the present rating rule and handicap allowance the best length seems to be about 16 ft. to 17 ft. on the waterline. It does seem also that if a boat is to be consistently successful no great departure can be made from the general proportions of the later sailing sixareens.

Some years ago after sailing a zulu boat in local regattas I was rash enough to plan a Shetland model, without reference to the great store of accumulated experience which was available. She was 18 ft. overall, 14 ft. 8 ins. on the waterline, 5 ft. 6½ ins. beam, and her mid draught was 1 ft. 6½ ins. With her ample beam she had good sail carrying capacity, but strange to say, and in spite of big sails she was slow in light winds.

She was followed by a second boat, planned from experience got from the first, but again without reference to standard practice. Of the same overall length she was 8 ins. shorter on the waterline, 2½ ins. less beam, and 3¾ ins. more draught. This was an improvement. On the same displacement she had a smaller wetted surface and was more weatherly under all conditions, and faster in light winds.

After sailing both these boats my son got out the drawing-board and produced a third boat. She was a couple of feet longer, and the mid-section a little further forward, and she has proved to be much the fastest and a good all-weather boat. Her lines are shown in Fig. 5 and she carries 205 sq. ft. of sail. This is perhaps rather on the large side for comfort, but the tax on sail area is small, and one can always reef.

But the point to note is that this boat has been much the most successful racer of the three, and that when her proportions were recently brought up to 30 ft. of overall length to compare with those of a sixareen this is what we find:—

	No. 8 of Table "Spinnoway" (Sixareen of 1889)	No. 5 of Table "Hope" (Model of Sixareen of 1910)	Above boat "Laughing Water"
Overall length	30 ft. 0 ins.	30 ft. 0 ins.	30 ft. 0 ins.
Waterline length	26 ft. 9 ins.	26 ft. 9 ins.	24 ft. 0 ins.
Height amidships	4 ft. 2 ins.	4 ft. 4 ins.	4 ft. 7 ins.
Freeboard amidships	1 ft. 10 ins.	1 ft. 10 ins.	1 ft. 10 ins.
Midship draught	2 ft. 4 ins.	2 ft. 6 ins.	2 ft. 9 ins.
Greatest beam	8 ft. 1 ins.	8 ft. 3 ins.	8 ft. 3 ins.
Waterline beam	7 ft. 1 ins.	?	7 ft. 3 ins.

This model has come back from the shallow beamy boat to quite near the proportions of the sailing sixareens, and she is markedly the best boat!

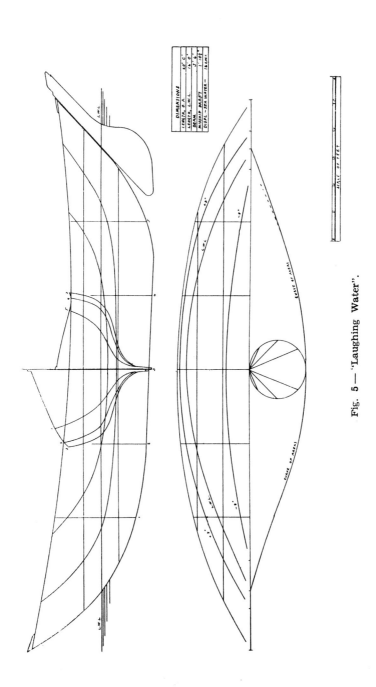

Fig. 5 — "Laughing Water".

Milestones in the development of the racing model in Shetland were the appearance of the "Still", the "Smugga" and "Miss Gadabout" by Walter Shewan of Fetlar. These boats gave a tremendous fillip to racing in the North Isles. Then came that marvellous pair the "Ripple" and "Mareel" by James Smith of Lerwick. The duels fought out between these boats by different builders stimulated racing in the twenties, and the same boats are still sailing and provide incentive to produce still better boats if this be possible.

Now there are the popular inter-club races held annually at Lerwick, for which any club may enter a team of two boats. This race bringing boats from all parts of the Islands together will do much to maintain the high standard both of boats and seamanship.

Chapter VIII.

SPEED AND SPEED ROSES

(The speed rose is a graphical method of showing the speed of a boat on all points of sailing).

THE fascinating thing about speed on the water is that it is related to the size of the craft, and that a 14-footer pressed to 6 knots can give an equal thrill to a 56-footer tearing before a rising gale at 12 knots, if indeed the latter could attain this speed.

In travelling through the water every displacement* craft creates a wave pattern which changes with her speed. As the speed increases the waves become longer and longer, and the energy required to form them greater and greater, until a point is reached at which the waves made by the passage of the boat through the water are of the same length, and moving with the same speed as the boat herself. Here she is constantly trying to push up a wave which she herself is making, and she becomes extremely hard to drive.

This point is commonly called the critical speed and is expressed by the formula "C" (in knots) equals 1.34 $\sqrt{\text{l.w.l.}}$, so that to compare the performance of craft of similar form but of different size, it is convenient to express the performance of each as a percentage of the "C" for her waterline. That is to say they are compared at speeds at which each make the same wave pattern round her hull, and conditions are dynamically similar.

In the case mentioned above the 14- and the 56-footer are each travelling at about 20% above their "C" and thus, if of the same model, will make similar wave patterns round their hulls, the only difference being that those made by the larger boats will be much larger. Even so the comparison begins to break down when the difference in size is great. This scale effect is referred to below.

Shetland boats are all very similar in general form, and how nearly their performance is related to waterline length is shown by the figures quoted in the last chapter, where the two leading boats each completed the whole regatta course at an average of 96% of their "C"s.

Though "C" is a very useful yardstick with which to compare any class of sailing craft it must be kept in mind that very large vessels are incapable of reaching their "C", while very small ones may frequently exceed it by 25%.

The fastest of the clipper ships, for example, could perhaps make up to 90% of their "C"s for short periods, while vessels in the 80-ft. to 100-ft. waterline

---

* Only displacement craft are being considered.

class could probably just about reach their "C" of 12 to 13½ knots respectively: "Britannia", for example, 86.8 ft. waterline, "C" 12.5 knots, recorded speed 12.5 knots. †

In 1935 the writer had a sail in the Banks schooner "Bluenose", when she was at Falmouth. She had a waterline length of 112 ft. and set off from the harbour with all her 10,000 square feet of sail set, but took in the fisherman staysail when the wind freshened. She was then said to be travelling at 13 knots, 92% of her "C". Her mainboom was 81 ft. long. Imagine gybing this ship in a fresh gale! In tacking she took 60 seconds from "helm down" till she filled on the other tack, having made a large circle of about nine points.

"Vega" with Stemhead Rig.

In crossing the Pacific, W. A. Robinson's 27½ ft. l.w.l. "Svaap" averaged 7.83 knots over a whole 24-hour period when running in strong trade winds. This was 11% over her "C", and to average this for 24 hours she must have exceeded it very considerably at times.

Returning now to the Shetland model boats we will examine such figures as are available.

In May 1950 the ex-racer "Calloo" of 18 ft. waterline, and converted to a cabin cruiser, made the passage from Rovi Head at the north entrance to Lerwick harbour to Uyeasound pier, a distance of 31.3 sea miles, in 4 hours 55 minutes. This gives an average speed of 6.36 knots, or 12% above the "C" for her waterline. On the 14-mile stretch from the southern extremity of Hunder Holm to the White Hill light the average speed was 6.6 knots, or 16% over "C". The wind was on the port quarter and off the land, and in strength touched 35 miles an hour in the squalls.

In the last chapter it was mentioned that a 16-ft. waterline racing boat averaged 6.7 knots, or 25% over her "C" on a free reach in sheltered water.

Some years ago a 14-ft. waterline boat built on the Hardanger Fjord (No. 3 of Table already published) with square sail rig, and with my daughter at the helm, covered 1890 yards in 8 minutes 50 seconds, giving a speed of 6.3 knots, which is also 25% over her "C".

Finally reference to Fig. 6 where the speed rose of "Vega", (a 14-ft. waterline Shetland boat) is given will show two points and dates on the port quarter of the rose where almost exactly the same speeds were got at sailing angles of 103 degrees and 107 degrees off the wind.

With regard to the best speeds recorded by Shetland fishing boats figures are naturally more difficult to get.

Mr Jas. Williamson, however, has given me particulars of a fast trip he made from Lerwick docks to the south entrance of Out Skerries, a distance of 20 sea miles. The boat was a 16-ft. keel fourareen and presumably 21-ft. to 21½-ft. waterline, and was skippered by Robert Humphray of Skerries. The wind was from S.W. and very strong, and the tows had to be worked frequently when the seas became dangerous. The time take was 2½ hours, and the speed was therefore 8 knots. The critical speed for 21½ ft. is 6.2 knots, so that the whole run was made at an average of 29% over the boat's "C".

Mr Ratter has given me particulars of a run made about 70 years ago by a Cullivoe sixareen from Lerwick docks to Cullivoe, a distance of 33½ sea miles. He got the particulars from the late Mr Magnus Sinclair who remembered the event clearly. The wind was very strong from S. to S.E. so that the sea must have been rough and the boat was well reefed down. The boat was skippered by George Spence of Cullivoe, and the time taken was 3½ hours, but as the tide was favourable and would make an appreciable difference in passing Whalsay Sound and in approaching Cullivoe, 2½ miles will be knocked off the distance, making it 31 miles actually sailed, and the average speed through the water 8.86 knots. The boat was of 20 ft. keel or say 27 ft. waterline so that the whole journey must have been made at a speed averaging 27% over her "C".

Finally we have the account of the sixareen returning from the haaf in the storm of 1881 and referred to in a previous chapter. For this, working from the information given, I arrived at a speed of 9¼ knots, or 30% over her "C".

We have therefore carefully timed records of 25% over "C" for three different boats under what one would describe as just good sailing conditions. They can be checked any day that the wind suits either in the same or in similar boats, as there is no reason to think that they are very unusual. And we have three less certain records going up to 29% or 30% for fishing sixareens or fourareens.

It is not very remarkable that these light shallow draught boats can so easily attain high speeds in sheltered waters, but it speaks volumes for the seaworthiness and balance of the sixareens, and the skill and daring of their crews, that they were driven at such speeds in the open sea and on coastal journeys.

These men knew their boats, and had complete confidence in them and in their own skill, and took pride in driving to the utmost of both.

When caught in a storm at sea there is reason to believe that the sixareen was considered safer scudding under sail than in any other way. In the remarkable account of the storm of 1881 given by Charles Johnson, from which passages have already been quoted, he makes it clear that the alternative to running for the land, if the skipper was unwilling to make a landfall on a lee shore, was to run off into deep water.

It was not blind scudding either. The boat was under perfect control as to speed, and to a large extent as to direction also, and this would help greatly in avoiding the most dangerous seas.

On this most interesting subject of the maximum speed that has been attained by normal displacement sailing craft at sea I venture the statements, that length for length, nothing could equal the square-sail-rigged sixareen, and that with sailing ships generally almost all the improvements of the last 100 years have been in ability to get to windward quickly—filling out the Speed Rose, in fact. In a light wind one of the J class racers could probably sail "on a bowline" at almost the speed of the wind itself, and it is in this direction that real improvement in performance has come.

Some years ago I made a diagram to represent the performance of a small Shetland boat on all points of sailing, and a daughter who had been sailing in the boat under test called this a "Speed Rose", and so an article under this title appeared in the *Yachting Monthly* of June, 1944.

Since then another small boat has been built to a modified design, and two speed roses are given for her in Fig. 6.

Ideally these tests should be made in the open sea in a steady wind and with accurate means of measuring wind speed, the angle of the course made good to the wind, and the speed through the water. But this presents difficulties in a small boat, and these speed roses were made in an almost tide-free harbour with adequate landmarks, and the actual courses sailed were determined from these. This method automatically corrects for leeway.

When the tests were completed the courses were laid out and measured on the largest scale Admiralty chart (9.67 ins. equal to 6080 ft.). The wind direction was taken as dividing the angle between successive tacks, so that where any appreciable change in direction occurred it would be noted.

The wind speed was measured by vane anemometer.

For the larger speed rose of Fig. 6, which is the result of a test made on the 8th July, 1949, the wind speed was measured on a low shore at 10 feet above sea level, and a short distance to windward of the sailing area. Readings of 1 minute duration were taken every 10 minutes, and all except two (one above and one below) lay between 10.5 and 11.1 knots.

The smaller speed rose is a composite one made up from figures got on two or three different days, but all in a light wind which was measured or estimated at about 6½ knots.

The tiny circles mark speed and course made good on the tack or quarter on which it is plotted, and the broken circles their image on the opposite tack or quarter.

A perpendicular dropped from any point on the sailing curve to the "dead to windward" line will give the speed that would be made good dead to windward when sailing that course.

In this case the best was 2.66 knots with a course made good of 53 degrees off the wind. A single reading got on the starboard tack does give a rather better figure but could have been the result of a small change in wind direction so it is not to be relied on. The broken line completes the curve where sailing was impossible.

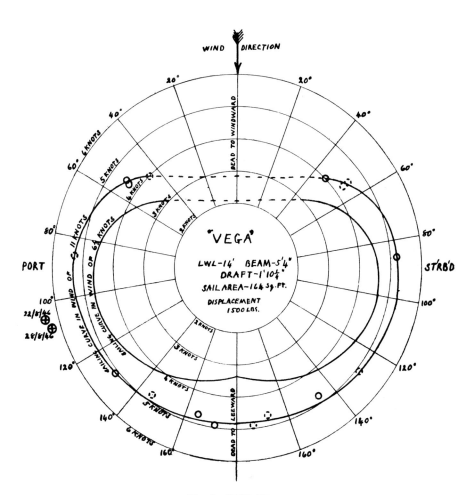

Fig. 6 — Speed Rose.

Looking at Fig. 6 it will be seen that the speed through the water increases very rapidly as the boat's head is eased, and with a course 73 degrees off the wind she reaches her critical speed in a wind of 11 knots, while a maximum speed of 5.3 knots is reached at 100 degrees off the wind. From this point the speed drops gradually to 4.8 knots when running dead.

In this case it is clear from the curve that if the mark is dead to lee nothing will be gained by running off first on one gybe and then on the other.

Looking at the curve for wind speed of 6½ knots, however, it will be seen that in this lighter wind the best speed dead to lee will be got by running about 20 degrees off on either side. This gives a speed dead to lee of 3.55 knots (the point where a straight edge touching the sailing curves cuts the "dead to leeward" line). Running straight in this wind she would only make 3.33 knots.

As a rough and ready rule one might say that any of these Shetland racing boats will beat dead to windward at at least one-half of her critical speed—say .7 √l.w.l—and that she will do this in almost any wind from 10 knots upwards to the point where the conditions of the sea prevent it.

In this chapter I have tried to show what performance can be expected from a boat of the Sheland model, and to bring out the relatively high speeds which the sixareens of these islands were capable of attaining. It is probably safe to say that no other type of boat was quite as fast, and at the same time as safe as these. Perhaps this is not very surprising, as the rivalry between the haaf boats was commented on in the early years of last century, and almost 100 years later the sixareen men of the North Isles still stressed this demand for boats that were light and fast as well as seaworthy, and these characteristics persist in their racing descendants.

A summary of the best recorded speeds of Shetland boats referred to in this and in previous chapters is given below.

Racers with gunter lug and jib:—

    14 ft. l.w.l. .... 6.4 knots
    16 ft. l.w.l. .... 6.7 knots

Half decked cruiser, gunter rigged:—

    18 ft. l.w.l. .... 6.6 knots

Fishing boats with square-sail (deduced from information given by fishermen):—

    21 ft. l.w.l. .... 8.0 knots
    27 ft. l.w.l. .... 8.8 knots
    28 ft. l.w.l. .... 9.2 knots

Having discussed at some length the speeds obtainable in Shetland model racing boats it may be interesting just to glance at a popular racing class yacht of not too different L.W.L. The Scandinavian-designed Dragon class is about 18 ft. L.W.L. and one of the best known among smaller yachts today.

Reports of the races held at Largs on 5th July, and at Hunter's Quay on 8th July, 1950, in fresh to strong winds, give sailing times of about 3 hours for the 13-mile Largs course and about 1 hr. 28 min. for the winner of the 7.15-mile course at Hunter's Quay. Both courses were triangular.

By and large the times taken by "Mareel" to sail the 9.4-mile course at Uyeasound in 1948, and by "Miss Gadabout" and "Laughing Water" in 1950, as recorded in the last chapter, do not seem to compare unfavourably with these.

Be this as it may, it is worth noting that these boats owe practically nothing to the theories of naval architecture. They have developed almost entirely from experience gathered over generations of contact with the sea in small craft, and trace their ancestry right back through the sixareens to the Viking ships of 1,000 years ago—perhaps to the even earlier Nydam boat built in the third century of the Christian era.

All were light-displacement undecked boats built for speed. All were double-ended with raked or curved stems and bold sheer; and all were clench-built. These are still the essential features of the Shetland boat today. In fact a sketch of the Nydam boat might almost pass for one of a Ness yole. The high sheer, raking stems and flared sides are the same, while something very like the kaeb and humlibaund was used in this ancient ship. The fastening too was by nails clenched on "rooves" and the tafts fitted over the timbers as they do in Shetland today.

But while all these craft have the same fundamental characteristics, each was adapted for a special purpose: the Oseberg ship as a queen's barge; the sixareen for lightness and safety at sea; and the racing model for speed under sail.

For this purpose the Shetland model boat has perhaps reached as high a stage of perfection as did her ancestors in their own spheres.

The End.